T0312808

To

....

From

....

DEVOTIONS

from the LAKE

CONTENTS

A Rocking Boat   10

Roasted Coffee Beans   13

Safety in the Waters   14

A New Song   17

Sailing Companions   19

Hearts by the Hearth   20

Skipping Stones   23

Mourning Doves   24

Stove-Top Lessons   26

A Well-Worn Dock   29

Bait Shop: Treasure Trove   30

Sunrise Expectancy   35

Record Player   36

Horseback Riding   38

Supernatural Snorkeling   41

Teatime   42

Berry Bushes   45

Homemade Popcorn   46

Lighten Your Load   49

Superb Sandwiches   50

Paw Prints   53

The Otters' Juggle   54

Hammock Rhythms   59

He Names the Stars   61

Butterfly Honey   62

Campsite Light   65

A Bright Cove   66

Fireflies   69

A Hawk's Freedom   70

A Big Rock   73

Tree Roots   74

Cloud Shapes   77

Spotless   78

Moments of Reflection   81

Summertime Tag	82	Gazebo Getaway	126
Fall Turnings	85	Flying on the Ground	129
Winter Charm	86	Hope Like Adrenalin	130
Spring Breakthrough	89	Bread and Butter	132
A Lesson from the Lake		Books Abound	135
Bottom	90	Tadpole Genetics	137
The Comeback Card	94	Playing Fetch	138
Puzzle Pieces	97	A Rare Shell	143
Reunion	98	Banquet on a Blanket	144
Drop Anchor	101	Marmot in a Meadow	146
Your Perfect Room	102	Flower Crowns and Stick	
Spiderweb Repellant	105	Swords	148
Brotherly Love	106	Camp Chair Prepared	151
Pure Rainbow	109	Blessings Versus Luck	152
Down to the Roots	110	Watercolor Life	155
Apple of God's Eye	113	The Dimensions of Love	156
Mountain Lion Mamas	114	Following in Jesus' Wake	159
Heart Health	118	Storing Acorns	160
Weeping Willows	121	Roly-Poly Armor	163
Lake Mirror	122	Grace as Sunscreen	166
God the Gardener	125	Flags of Identity	169

Constellation Connections	170	First-Aid Kit	199
Where the Sky Meets the Ground	173	Spring Salad	200
		Tiptoes	203
Ski Tricks	174	Midnight Snack	204
Muffin Munchers	177	Follow the Leader	207
Fish Out of Water	178	Fishing-Rod Patience	208
Nap in Grace	181	Ice-Cream Drops	211
Life Preserver	182	Bonfire Friends	212
Moonbeams	185	Stillness of a Heron	215
Traveling in Harmony	186	When Life Moves Too Fast	216
Beach Paradise	191	The Misnamed Dragonfly	219
Robin's Egg Blue	192	Fish Fry	220
Watermelon Smiles	195	The Golden Hour	223
Diving into Decisions	196		

A ROCKING BOAT

[Jesus] said to them, "Let us go across to the other side of the
lake." So they set out, and as they sailed he fell asleep.

Luke 8:22–23 esv

O ut on the lake in a small wooden boat, lying on a blanket, book in hand,
you glance up at the still skies and tree trunks lining the bank. The only
sound is the rustling of the trees' leaves as a steady wind starts a ripple of easy
waves that gently rock the boat. A calmness covers you, and the rhythmic lap-
ping of the water and the warmth of the lake air draw you into drowsiness. Is it
any wonder Jesus fell asleep in a boat?

When we allow ourselves time and space to connect and rest with the
Father, He gives us His promised peace and steady strength to face whatever the
day brings. Like our days, an afternoon on the lake can hold uncertain circumstances. A storm could roll in, carrying us somewhere we never planned to go.
And sometimes resting feels irresponsible. But even the King of creation slept in
a boat. Even He gave Himself permission to rest in nature. We have permission
to rest safely beside Him.

Lord, thank You for being in my boat with me. Please give me the
faith that allows me to relax by Your side in any situation. Amen.

ROASTED COFFEE BEANS

We are the aroma of Christ.

2 CORINTHIANS 2:15 ESV

Certain foods carry specific scents that can transport us to a memory or draw kids in from their play at dinnertime. But freshly brewed coffee is something all its own. It has an *aroma*, like a bouquet of unique scents blooming and melding into one delicious smell in the air.

For the first person to wake up, the house is still. Shuffling in slippers to the kitchen, you notice the early morning light glowing through the window, the lake still sleeping. This is a wonderful moment: you open a new bag of coffee beans, pour them into the grinder, and rouse the world with the whirl of each bean blasting into tiny bits. Then as the coffee brews, its fragrance carries through the house, pleasantly waking the rest of the family and drawing them, one by one, to the kitchen.

Family is meant to be a combination of personas, each with his or her own fragrance that brings a one-of-a-kind flavor to the blend. Through a coffee roast's aroma, connoisseurs can distinguish its unique flavors, from hints of caramel to cherry undertones. In the same way, when God surrounds us, the warmth of His love causes an aroma to arise, revealing the unique attributes of Christ in us and awakening the world to experience His glory today.

Father, You brilliantly designed coffee beans to wake us up and bring us comfort. In the same way, help us to carry Your sweet, bold aroma to each other and the rest of the world. Amen.

SAFETY IN THE WATERS

By wisdom a house is built, and by understanding it is established . . .
the rooms are filled with all precious and pleasant riches.

PROVERBS 24:3–4 ESV

If you look closely at a beavers' lodge on a chilly day, you may see a wisp of vapor rising through the top. It's the beavers' breath. Through the masterful design of twigs and logs glued together by mud, the beavers have left an opening at the peak, like a chimney, for air to ventilate through. Inside, the close-knit beaver family sleeps.

Beavers strategically build sturdy wooden homes surrounded by water. Like a castle's moat, the water offers protection from predators, with secret entrances located underneath. Water is life for the beaver family: a drinking source, a food bank, and a water park where the kits splash around and play. It's a safe and humble home for a rich family life.

God extends the invitation to build our homes here and now, surrounded and kept by the eternal waters flowing from heaven's streams. Out in His waters, we are protected and given everything we need, from food on the table to nourishment for our souls. Here, God's design for wealth in this life meets us in the form of close bonds created in our family and friendships, treasures that will outlast time.

Father, give me the wisdom to build my home on Your living
waters, where You protect and care for me. Help me treasure
Your love and the gift of my relationships above all. Amen.

A NEW SONG

Oh sing to the LORD a new song;
sing to the LORD, all the earth!

PSALM 96:1 ESV

On an early morning at the lake, the inhabitants of the house are sleeping soundly in rooms filled with serene silence. Outside the world is waking up to an orchestra comprised of crickets, frogs, and birds. It's a symphony of praise to God before any human mind turns His way.

Birds and insects in this natural band have specific songs God has given them to sing. Crickets chirp, frogs croak, and even birds, with their more varied vocal ranges, croon their own tunes.

Here is one beautiful way we differ from the rest of creation: God has given us freedom and creativity. When we feel stuck in a rut spiritually or bound by boredom of routine in our lives, we can dig deep and start singing something completely new. Let's join the natural band members in the morning and blend our voices with theirs. The Father receives glory when we let go of the past and move on to the new melodies with fresh depths of wisdom and lyrics of praise.

God, wake me up each day with a new song to sing
to You. Don't let me stick to songs of the past, but
help me find praises for the future. Amen.

SAILING COMPANIONS

*When he got into the boat, his disciples followed him. And
behold, there arose a great storm on the sea.*

MATTHEW 8:23–24 ESV

Windy days beckon friends out for sailing on the lake. Each person takes a position on the sailboat–one at starboard, another at the stern, and another at port side. As they steer, call out directions, and hold the rope that steadies the sail, the boat moves forward, cutting through the water, picking up pace.

But then–a raindrop.

The same wind that inspired the adventure brings clouds. Your heart skips a beat with each *plop* of water landing around you. Everyone scrambles to steady the now swaying boat. Looking behind, you realize you are already too far from shore to head back.

When storms come in life, it's natural to panic and doubt whether God is in control. But don't bail at the early signs of a squall! Jesus hasn't called us out of the boat, but to the other side of the shore. God gives us friends in our boats to help navigate rough waters. Jesus reaches out to us in storms through the helping hands of our friends. He will be there to calm the waters, sooner or later, and the companionship created through the journey will carry us on through the next.

*Jesus, when waves rock my boat, remind me of the friends
You've placed in my life to embrace the adventure alongside
me. Remind me that You, the One who commands the
waves and wind, will never leave me alone. Amen.*

HEARTS BY THE HEARTH

I remind you to fan into flame the gift of God.

2 Timothy 1:6 esv

Icicles hang from the roofline of the porch, reflecting the sun like crystal lights. Frost frames the windowsills. Inside, the fireplace draws all the lakehouse guests around its inviting heat. The fire inside the brick hearth glows and crackles, radiating hot waves that chase away the cold. The tides of comfort spread out over your chest and sink into your heart. Heat from the hearth circulates through your body, defrosting every part. You relax. You smile.

God's gift of His presence is an inviting glow that draws us in and fills us with warmth. The heat starts in our chests, reaches our hearts, and then ignites the rest of us. Sometimes we stray to colder places further from His presence, and our hearts carry in frost from the outside world. In His presence they thaw, and we become warmhearted again.

If the fire dwindles in the hearth, fan it with a newspaper or blow into the embers, and it will blaze again. When we pull up close to God, just one whisper of His name and His flame rises and chases away the cold. When icicles hang outside and frost forms on the windows, inside His presence is always within reach so we can drape it over us like a blanket by the fireplace.

Father, thank You for the gift of Your presence that beckons me in from the cold. I place myself before Your fireplace; keep my heart kindled. Amen.

SKIPPING STONES

Cast all your anxiety on him because he cares for you.

1 PETER 5:7

Skipping rocks across water requires a touch of playfulness. Chances are, if you launch a rock haphazardly up in the air, it will arc back down, make a splash, and sink to the lake floor. For a stone to skip, it needs a lightness in the toss as it's released over the water.

What motivates someone to stop and skip a stone? First, it's fun to see how many times you can get it to hop across the water before sinking. It's also an idea that springs from a carefree place in our hearts: we skip stones when we're relaxed and ambling beside a lake, maybe chatting with a loved one. It requires little concentration, so we mindlessly pick up stones and send them flying over the water, just for fun.

Anxiety blocks this carefree part of us. The weight of worry keeps us from believing we can stop to enjoy some of the simple pleasures that make us happy. God wants us to cast *all* our anxieties on Him the way we toss rocks over water. Erasing anxiety might also look like reading a book, writing in a journal, creating arts and crafts, or taking a bubble bath by candlelight. Let Jesus carry your cares when they trouble you, and find the freedom to skip some stones.

Jesus, I admit I often try to carry my concerns on my own. Remind me to toss them to You and enjoy the activities that lighten my heart when I need a lift. Amen.

MOURNING DOVES

Surely he has borne our griefs
and carried our sorrows.

ISAIAH 53:4 ESV

I n the morning and evening times, the soothing call of mourning doves echoes across the lake from the surrounding woodlands. The sound of their *coo-woo-woo* carries to the lake house's front porch. It is a mournful yet sweet sound. Sometimes we face sorrows in our lives deeper than words or even tears can express; the missing pieces in our hearts due to loved ones' passing on from this life can draw us to silence. When nature offers up sounds of mourning for us, it is a comfort. We let the doves' voices speak for ours, and we realize it is okay to feel sadness for a time.

Besides perching on branches of trees, mourning doves are commonly found sitting on telephone wires. This reminds us that when mourning stirs anew, we can find comfort in a phone call to a friend who understands or to a person who experiences the heartache with us. Sharing memories with trusted friends and family can bring deeper healing and a more cherished remembrance.

In these moments, we more deeply grasp the reality of heaven, where our loved ones are held. In the meantime, Jesus carries our sorrows and bears our grief with us. When the mourning doves call, we feel our grief, then release it to Him. He reminds us of a better time coming when we will all be reunited with Him.

Father, when grief arises, help me feel it, share it, and release it to You and the friends and family You've placed in my life. Through harder times, let the reality of heaven bring comfort in the sorrow. Amen.

STOVE-TOP LESSONS

The LORD is compassionate and gracious,
slow to anger, abounding in love.

PSALM 103:8

Stoves are the hub of the home, the centerpiece of any lake-house kitchen. Turn the dial or light the burner and in moments its heat waves rise through the pot, cooking your creation and blending the flavors into a mealtime masterpiece. Besides cooking us delicious meals, stoves have been useful for teaching children a singular lesson through time: that some areas of life are off-limits and can cause us harm. What parent hasn't warned his or her child not to touch a hot stove top?

Often, though, the child touches it anyway. Then the parent is there to rinse the burn with cool water and apply ointment and a bandage. The parent's compassion leads him or her to comfort from the shock of pain and help heal the wound.

Later in life, we choose to touch other "hot stove tops" that God has warned us to avoid. Curiosity gets the best of us or we just want to do things our way. When this happens and we get hurt, our Father is not quick to anger. In fact, His parental instincts lead Him to draw us near into a comforting hug and to bring us healing in time. We learn at these times not only that "stove tops" really are dangerous, but that He loves us even when we fail to listen. Our trust grows, and next time we can choose to obey.

Father, thank You for the guidelines You give me in Your Word for my life. When I mess up, help me know that You are not angry but willing to comfort me and heal me when I'm hurt. Amen.

A WELL-WORN DOCK

I have fought the good fight, I have finished the race, I have kept the faith.

2 TIMOTHY 4:7 ESV

Stepping out from the lakeshore onto a dock, you hear the wood, worn by shoes and the elements, creak beneath your feet. Giving way to your weight and the waves, the dock bobs up and down. This path onto the water may seem rickety—bolts rusted and wood frayed. At first, doubts may surface about the reliability of the dock's support. But with each step forward, plank by plank, you gain confidence as you feel its sturdiness holding you up. Your fear transforms into trust in the dependability of a dock visitors have counted on for years.

Any path onto water takes faith, whether it's faith in the wood planks and nails or in the buoyancy of a partial bridge held up by air-filled barrels. Faith is the sturdy bridge we use to cross over occasional swells and waves that threaten to draw us into the water. When the seemingly fragile pieces creak under our troubles and pressures, we are surprised to see that once again, they're holding us up above the water!

We read in Hebrews 11 how the saints of the past walked this well-worn path of faith and finished well. Their example encourages us to keep going, even if a neighbor's renovated, freshly waxed dock looks more appealing. Ours is a humble course forward, but it is sturdy and can be trusted.

> *God, show me the well-used bridges of faith to walk*
> *in this life. I trust You to enable me to walk humbly*
> *over the waters, borne up by faith. Amen.*

BAIT SHOP: TREASURE TROVE

*"Truly I tell you, anyone who will not receive the kingdom
of God like a little child will never enter it."*

LUKE 18:17

For little boys and girls, a trip inside the bait shop on a dock is a look inside the treasure trove of fishing aids. It's a place that's not boring but alive, full of hiding places, strange smells, and interesting gadgets. The fishing tackle looks like tiny, colorful toys. The scent of wet wood and earthy insects hints at fun-filled, messy adventures ahead. Peeking over a chirping wooden box, a child stares wide-eyed as the father opens the lid, exposing all kinds of crickets crawling and skipping around the inside of the chest.

Children have the amazing ability to see the world through the eyes of wonder. Everything is new, and whatever delight comes to them they receive freely; they don't insist on earning it. God has prepared His kingdom for us as a gift. We cannot work to be good enough to deserve it. We are asked to become like children, with wonder-filled eyes and hearts, our hands open to receive the kingdom He offers.

If even a bait shop can contain treasures, how much more the kingdom God has created for us!

*Father, teach me again how to be like a child before
You. I want to receive Your kingdom as a gift in awe
and gratitude for all You've prepared for me. Amen.*

SUNRISE EXPECTANCY

The path of the righteous is like the light of dawn,
which shines brighter and brighter until full day.

PROVERBS 4:18 ESV

Hopes to catch the sunrise draw the sleepiest of us out of our beds and to the lakeside horizon. Looking out from the shore, we see deep purples swell above the distant edge of the dark waters. Time brings gradual changes in the sky. Slowly the sky begins to lighten with shades of pink. As the golden drop of sun draws up out of the water, the pink brightens and flashes of orange appear across the great expanse. Beholding this view, we dismiss the sleep lost and experience renewed energy brought by the dawn.

When we are young, we envision big dreams for our lives, many inspired by the heart and mind of God. God Himself dreamed up sunsets and imagined the world. Then He created us for divine plans and purposes. If He seems slow on delivery of your dreams, keep watching the horizon—another sunrise is on the way. His plans move forward at the start of every new day, and we will watch them unfold, growing brighter and brighter until complete. We don't have to lose sleep over the disappointments and failures we inevitably face in life.

If you are stuck between the beginning and the fulfillment of a dream, keep your eye on the sky. Let each sunrise remind you of God's creativity and power, and stay hopeful.

Father, Your sunrises remind me of Your faithfulness
to complete Your good plans for my life. Give me
patience when the sun seems slow to reach full day, as
I watch the horizon with joyful expectancy. Amen.

RECORD PLAYER

[Speak] to one another with psalms, hymns, and songs from the
Spirit. Sing and make music from your heart to the Lord.

EPHESIANS 5:19

Grandparents' lake houses hold the charm of the past, particularly ones built like cabins with wooden beams, stone fireplaces, and wraparound porches with rocking chairs. The rustic qualities carry with them the nostalgia of the decades paired with the hospitality of home.

Inside in a corner of the living room sits an old record player. Records still play during daily activities, while a grandparent cooks, after a family meal, or while young and old lounge together around the fireplace. Records are switched out from jazz hits of the 1920s to calming classical tunes to your grandparents' favorite hymns. Whatever the genre, the melodies and lyrics are a backdrop to some of the best moments spent together at the lake house.

Music connects us to memories and provides a soundtrack to our lives. Moments are strung together within the medleys, and a poetic sweetness sounds in our shared stories. In these rustic homes the tunes played may be modern or musty with age, but they bind us together in ways nothing else can, and our lives lived together become a song that reaches the ears of God.

Father, let the soundtrack of our lives connect us to You. Amen.

HORSEBACK RIDING

Be not like a horse or a mule, without understanding,

which must be curbed with bit and bridle,

or it will not stay near you.

PSALM 32:9 ESV

Horses are often skittish, sometimes brazen and strong-willed, and always beautiful creatures. Riding in a saddle, the reins in your grasp, you can guide a trained horse through trails in the woods. Horseback riding connects us with nature as the *clip-clop* of the horse's hooves reverberates through the trees. The horse knows which way to go by the direction you pull on the reins. The bit and bridle form smooth lines of communication between you and the animal transporting you.

But the bit and the bridle aren't always necessary. If you've developed a relationship with the horse, a deep understanding and instincts about how to "steer" him, you can now go horseback riding without the saddle and the reins. Relying upon just the bond between you, you and the horse are in sync, and you guide the animal with gentle tugs on its mane, a soft word of direction, and pressure from your right or left foot. The horse understands and responds to your touch.

God prefers that we develop a profound relationship with Him in which He can direct our paths by gentle nudges and kind whispers. No harsh words or tugs on an uncomfortable "bit"; we know how our Father "steers" us and we respond to His touch. When we are in sync, words are rarely needed, yet our lines of communication are smooth and clear. We naturally know and move according to

His will. When we choose nearness to God, this peaceful, rhythmic relationship is possible. Let us stay close to our Maker.

God, I want to be close to You so I will turn
at Your gentlest nudge. Amen.

SUPERNATURAL SNORKELING

I will give you hidden treasures,
riches stored in secret places.

ISAIAH 45:3

Doesn't everyone look a little silly in a snorkeling mask? The suctioned mask flattens the face inside and squishes the cheeks on the outside with the nose encased in a little plastic protruding triangle. Then there's the breathing tube jutting out of the mouth, sticking straight up in the air.

As funny as a snorkeler may look, this equipment allows him or her to do something supernatural: breathe under water. Because of this feat, we are able to discover whole new worlds of natural treasures, from kelp forests to rainbow trout and schools of minnows.

We may also appear silly to others when we're walking with Jesus. He may ask us to go somewhere or try something new that makes us stand out from "normal" people. We might choose to get up early for church instead of sleeping in. We may choose to read our Bibles as often as we read popular novels. But these "odd" little choices add up to big results: when we step out in faith or make little decisions that prioritize godly living, God gives us the ability to do the impossible, such as hear from heaven or witness a miracle of provision. Looking odd sometimes is worth experiencing the treasures of His kingdom and promises fulfilled that only He can orchestrate.

Jesus, help me to care more about what You think than
what others think about me. I want to experience the
hidden treasures of Your kingdom and promises. Amen.

TEATIME

He had to be made . . . fully human in every way, in order that he might
become a merciful and faithful high priest in service to God.

Hebrews 2:17

Afternoon tea on an overcast, dreary day settles us into the tranquility of moments spent indoors. Like the weather, teas have the remarkable ability to modify our moods. Green and black teas have antioxidants that can lift our spirits and steady our energy levels. Rooibos teas are being studied for their health attributes. Their caffeine-free draughts waft earthy scents as you sip, so you feel as if you are drinking from a cup of calm. Herbal teas can transfer us to relaxing tropical places with their flowery, fruity scent medleys rising in the steam to our faces.

While there are vast varieties of teas, our emotional spectrum is even broader. We feel sorrow and sadness, fear, hope, elation, and contentment to the heights and depths. Each emotion is a gift from God that allows us to express ourselves and can make us aware of the state of our hearts. If sometimes our feelings flow out of control, we know that Jesus has experienced the whole range of emotion and is able to help us from a place of understanding. He steadies our hearts and grounds them in His unchanging love.

He knows which kind of "tea" we need for any season or emotional state. If we need calming, He will comfort us with His presence. If we need joy and extra energy while battling depressing thoughts, He offers us deep belief in His goodness and plans to give us a hopeful future. If we need to get away from the stress of our everyday routine, He invites us to come away with Him and spend time praying and receiving from heaven, better than any tropical paradise on earth. If your emotions are as unpredictable as the weather outside, sit down with Jesus and process your heart's longings over a cup of your favorite tea.

Jesus, help me surrender my emotions to You so
I can feel known and understood. Amen.

BERRY BUSHES

The fruit of the Spirit is love, joy, peace, patience, kindness,
goodness, faithfulness, gentleness, self-control.

GALATIANS 5:22–23 ESV

As a tree is known by its fruit, a bush is known by its berries. Strawberries, blackberries, and raspberries all grow in the wild. If you're fortunate enough to happen across a hidden blackberry bush, pick the berries and take them back to the lake house for rinsing. Enjoy them in a salad or save them for morning cereal. The spurt of seeds and sweet juice as you bite into the dark purple berry is a delicious addition to your chosen dish.

Wouldn't it be convenient if growing the fruit of the Spirit in our lives were as simple as picking berries off a bush? Pick some patience and add it to your basket. You might want some more joy in there as well. How about a bushel of self-control for the road? It would definitely be easier, but once you picked the fruit off of its branch, eventually it would start to decay. It doesn't stay alive on its own.

Instead, God grows the fruit of the Spirit from within us where He abides. It's not as easy, as sometimes this requires pruning the parts of us that are not healthy. He is patient with us as these less desirable parts die and the good fruit blossoms. This fruit is the lasting kind that adds a sweetness to a life enjoyed with God.

God, please grow and nurture in me the
fruit of Your Spirit. Amen.

HOMEMADE POPCORN

Godliness with contentment is great gain.

1 Timothy 6:6

Movie nights at the lake house create excitement among the family. Everyone gathers in the living room. One sibling chooses three films and everyone can vote. In the mix are an action film, a romantic comedy, and a classic. The choice will set the tone of the evening and what emotions will be felt and shared among everyone watching. One parent gets the DVD player ready, and you walk into the kitchen to make the popcorn.

Making popcorn from scratch is a lost art. Try it! The kernels wiggle and hop in the pan until *pop!* the first kernel bursts through the hard shell like white cotton blooming in fast-forward. The first one signals all the others to follow as popping plays loudly in the air. Melt real butter on the stove and pour it over the popcorn. Then add a creative blend of your favorite popcorn seasoning and grated parmesan. The whole family will agree it tastes better than the stuff you get at the movie theater.

Movies are fun and bring families together. The kind of romance, drama, and action we watch in films can be appealing, and we may even be tempted to model our lives after those of the characters on the screen. But films are scripted and the products of writers' imaginations. Real life may be slower paced, but it can be exciting and adventurous if we model ourselves after godly people and Jesus Himself. Check the Bible for accounts of righteous people (such as Abraham or Paul) who led amazing and dramatic lives. Cinema stories can inspire us, but they can never replace the joy and thrill of a godly life well lived and savored, like a film night and a bucket of popcorn with the family.

God, Your script for my life is deeper and richer than any film meant for entertainment. Flavor my life with Your character and adventure. Amen.

LIGHTEN YOUR LOAD

"My yoke is easy and my burden is light."

When the kids are out of school for the summer, families escape for weeks at a time to a lake house. This longer-term vacation means that the chores of everyday life are part of the trip. Take laundry, for instance: the lake environment provides plenty of opportunities for the family to get their clothes dirty, whether it's ketchup from last night's burger cookout or mud from wading along the shoreline. Either way, the laundry piles up in each room and eventually, although it is vacation time, someone has to put the clothes in the wash.

Simple tasks and daily duties are a necessary part of the fabric of our lives. This fabric can get bogged down with dirt and make life feel heavy. The One who created the fabric offers to do our laundry. We can hand Him the material of our lives, and He will lift it into His presence to clean it and make it like new. Freshly washed and dried clothes feel lighter and carry a refreshing scent. So do our freshly laundered lives.

*God, thank You for offering to scrub my soul when
it gets weighed down by dirt and stains. I trust
You to make me clean and refreshed. Amen.*

SUPERB SANDWICHES

May the God of hope fill you with all joy and peace as you trust in him,
so that you may overflow with hope by the power of the Holy Spirit.

ROMANS 15:13

Fillers are an essential part of a superb sandwich. In the morning, all present choose what main ingredients they want in their sandwiches. Whether it's turkey, roast beef, cheese, or vegetables, the fillers–cheddar or provolone, hummus, pickles, potato chips, you name it–are what make the sandwich sing!

Later, in the boat out on the lake, everyone has sunbathed, swum, and climbed rocks. The glow of gladness is apparent on every face, and the elation of the day is at its peak. Then the group members realize that they all are famished. It's time to get out the sandwiches.

One at a time the sandwiches are removed from the cooler and passed to the appropriate persons. Someone gets out the chips, fruit, sodas, and iced tea, and as the lake smorgasbord is cheerfully consumed, stomachs stop rumbling as mouths are munching. The ingredients that filled the sandwiches now fill you up to satisfaction.

At the beginning of each day, we have the choice of what we are going to fill ourselves up with, what ingredients we'll add to work, hobbies, or church. Throughout the day we pour out our energies for those we love, and we will need to be filled again. Joy and peace are not just happy concepts, but part of the true sustenance of heaven. The same way fillers make key ingredients more flavorful and feed our stomachs, additives like joy and peace satisfy and sustain us at our cores, where we find new energy for the day ahead. Let's be wise about the way we build our "sandwiches."

God, thank You for fillers for my soul. Throughout my day, as I pour out for others, help me to choose joy and peace to fill me up again. Amen.

PAW PRINTS

Jesus said to him, "Have you believed because you have seen me?
Blessed are those who have not seen and yet have believed."

JOHN 20:29 ESV

Y ou're walking along the lakeside when you spot an indentation in the dirt that halts you in your tracks. It's a hefty, irregular circle with five smaller circles lining the top. A bear's paw print! A bear has been taking a stroll down by the water! In bewilderment, awe, and a touch of healthy fear you scan the area quickly, but the bear left hours ago. It's amazing to realize that your family and this wild animal are sharing the same area.

There are times when we want God to send us a sign that He is with us. God will often give us a sign if we need it, but when we believe simply by faith, we bless God and ourselves. God is pleased by our belief in Him. Sure, it might be easier if He would place bear-sized hints and signs along the path to prove He's near, but then we would not need to draw as close to Him, trusting Him to fill our lives with His presence whether we can spot His tracks or not.

Jesus, teach me to walk so near You that our
tracks in the dirt are side by side. Amen.

THE OTTERS' JUGGLE

"Seek first the kingdom of God and his righteousness,
and all these things will be added to you."

Matthew 6:33 esv

O tters are playful critters we love to watch, whether in a zoo or a natural habitat like a lake or stream. They splash, snicker, and cuddle, and we "oooh," "ahh," and clap. One of the otters' most curiously cute pastimes is juggling rocks. They will lie on their backs on a big rock, pick up a sizable pebble, and toss it back and forth, up in the air, and around in a circle. It's almost too adorable to take!

Otters have the ability to juggle just one rock at a time, and they are perfectly content with that. We, on the other hand, often feel as though we have to pick up and juggle all the parts of our lives. But God has made us to handle just one main priority, and that's seeking His kingdom and His righteousness. We may worry that if we juggle just this one "rock," we'll drop all the other important rocks and disaster will result. But Jesus promises that when we seek God's kingdom first–keep just that one rock in the air–then the rest will fall into place. Like otters, we can enjoy juggling the one thing that really matters and cause people to wonder at our happiness.

Jesus, I want life to be fun and full. Help me trust You with
every "rock" in my life so I can focus my energies on the
one that matters most: seeking Your kingdom. Amen.

HAMMOCK RHYTHMS

You hem me in, behind and before,
and lay your hand upon me.

PSALM 139:5 ESV

Hammocks are swings for grown-ups. Securing each end around a tree in the backyard of the lake house, you crawl in and stretch out. The hammock rocks back and forth, and you glide with the wind, cradled inside. Because you are in motion, your perspective is different: the sky, clouds, and trees seem to sway with you. Even though you are moving, you are in a state of rest and relaxation because you know the hammock is holding you snugly.

When life feels static, we sometimes match its lack of momentum and give way to a lazy lifestyle. Or we stress and take charge, possibly running ahead of ourselves and God. But there is another way. It's choosing the lifestyle along the rhythms of heaven, where hurry does not exist, yet activities and life beat forward in steady, harmonious praise to God. It may feel like a slower pace, but it allows time for praying intentionally and seeking wise counsel about our steps forward. Then, once we do move, even if it feels like an insignificant step God moves with us, our perspective is different, and we see that He causes situations to shift in our favor. The point is to start moving.

Then, even though we are in motion, we are also at rest. Like a hammock, God holds us safely in His care.

Lord, teach me a lifestyle matched to heaven's rhythms.
Walk with me as I pray and consider my path, and
let me see You at work around me. Amen.

HE NAMES THE STARS

He determines the number of the stars
and calls them each by name.

PSALM 147:4

S itting on a blanket under the sky's dark canvas dusted with stars makes us feel minuscule. What an expansive stellar display! They twinkle and wink down at us as if they know galactic secrets we haven't yet discovered. Even astronomers cannot count the number of stars in our galaxy. The Milky Way is estimated to hold one hundred billion–maybe more–of these gigantic balls of hot gas. That's just one galaxy in the universe!

God not only numbers the stars, both made and still forming, but He names them all, every last one. God has an affinity for giving identity. As much as He delights in naming the stars, He is even more concerned about giving each human being a name and identity. The stars reflect an aspect of His glory, but we are His very own. He has placed a part of Himself in us to shine out to the world. Even in our smallness, especially in comparison to the rest of the universe, we can part the darkness with His presence. He calls us by name and confers upon us the dignity of being His own eternal creation. How's that for a majestic reality? We're not as minuscule as we thought!

Father, when I feel lost in the vastness of time and space,
remind me of my unique identity in You. Call me by name,
and I will shine bright in my spot here in the world. Amen.

BUTTERFLY HONEY

How sweet are your words to my taste,
sweeter than honey to my mouth!

PSALM 119:103 ESV

Toward the end of a trail, you happen upon a garden of native plants and wildflowers bedecked with butterflies, lifting off from flowers and alighting upon others. It's a whimsical sight as wings of yellow, orange, and bright blue flutter around the garden. When a big, blue morpho butterfly touches down on a flower, draw closer and you can see it unravel its tongue-like appendage into the flower center. It works like a straw to draw up nectar from the flower. The liquid is as sweet and sticky as honey.

God's words and precepts are like honey to the soul. They issue from love and a pure heart. God's words are true, lovely, and right; His precepts offer guarding guidance that keeps us safe. When we taste His words and take them in, our hearts are uplifted like the blissful blue butterfly.

Butterflies survive on this nectar. It is their primary food source. The words of God are the key source of nourishment for our souls. They are not the kind of sweet that makes you feel sickly if you have too much. Enjoy–you can consume as much as you like! God's words are readily available and always gushing honey we can never get enough of.

Father, when I try to get my fill elsewhere in life,
bring me to the Bible where I can partake of Your
words that are as delightful as honey. Amen.

CAMPSITE LIGHT

We know that if the earthly tent we live in is destroyed, we have
a building from God, an eternal house in heaven.

2 CORINTHIANS 5:1

Campsites are temporary landing spots where we can unload our packs and gear and set ourselves up to experience life close to the earth, connected to nature. At first these sites are just trees, rocks, bushes, grass, and fresh air. But as everyone works to set up the tents, sleeping bags, firewood, and cooking utensils, the natural area turns into an interim home. The work pays off as you enjoy a meal camp-side, sitting on logs and rocks, taking in the beauty around you. The wilderness seems to welcome you as you make this spot your own.

There is something freeing about living light, the way we do when camping. The things we carry with us are mostly necessities, and the enjoyment of friendship and natural things are what we cherish in these moments. If our tents are blown down by strong winds, we are not devastated because we know we have a lasting house back in our neighborhood.

When we live lightly, keeping only essential possessions, we are free to enjoy companionship with our friends and family. If the wind threatens to knock down the lives we build here and now, we encourage each other to keep looking to our eternal dwelling in heaven. Our houses here are but lovely campsites—we're on our way to homes that will last forever.

Jesus, show me how to live lightly so I will keep my
eyes on my eternal home in heaven. Amen.

A BRIGHT COVE

Whatever is true, whatever is noble, whatever is right, whatever is pure,
whatever is lovely, whatever is admirable . . . think about such things.

PHILIPPIANS 4:8

Out in the middle of a lake cove, you float on your back, lazily moving your arms above your head and back down to your sides with the water rippling through your fingers. You kick your feet lightly, synchronizing with your waving arms. In this exquisite, encased space in nature, no bad thought can sink your heart. You float above anything that might drag you down.

This circle of water cut into the lake's bank creates an oasis. The opening in the tree line allows for the sun rays to beam down into the cove. Where light hits the blues of the water and greens of the leaves, the colors are highlighted; the scene sparkles. While you're free-floating and weightless in the water, happy thoughts keep your heart lifted and cheerful.

Our minds can be like a bright cove, an oasis filled with God's light. When our thoughts are highlighted by His Holy Spirit, darker places can be edged out. Focusing our thoughts on whatever is commendable, true, lovely, and pure keeps our minds in happiness and our hearts afloat.

God, brighten my mind with Your light and
presence so it becomes an oasis of thoughts focused
on the true qualities of heaven. Amen.

FIREFLIES

The light shines in the darkness, and the darkness has not overcome it.

JOHN 1:5

Fireflies are the lantern bugs of the evening, dazzling us from the porch with a light show. Tiny floating globes rise across the grass, around the bushes, and up trees. First-time viewers of the spectacle marvel at these flashing insects of the night.

Another name for the firefly is *lightning bug*, named after the physical phenomenon that cracks through the sky during a thunderstorm. One second the earth seems to be swallowed in darkness, and then with a flash, the entire nighttime sky lights up. This same sky light inspired humans' invention of electricity, which brightens civilization from murky street corners to rooms in a lake house.

We have always been fascinated by light, energized by its ability to dispel darkness in an instant. The world around us may dim, but the inkier the night, the brighter the light. Even minuscule insects brighten up the evening. God's light is greater than a cosmic combination of all the light in creation, powerful enough to light the gloomiest instances we face. We can look around nature, the sky, and even our street corners and find light that reminds us of a Power that never goes out.

Father, thank You for reminders in nature of light that overcomes darkness. I praise You for Your power to brighten up any circumstance in my life. Amen.

A HAWK'S FREEDOM

Now the Lord is the Spirit, and where the Spirit of the Lord is, there is freedom.

2 CORINTHIANS 3:17

Hawks glide on the wind, circling widely above the treetops in a freedom found only in the sky. If the hawk tried to hunt through the forest's trees, its vision would be limited and the branches and vines would entangle it. Instead, as warm air rises, it catches the bird's spread wings and lifts the hawk up in the air to soar over the forest with a bird's-eye view.

In our humanity, we can sometimes feel as though we're navigating treetops full of branches and vines that try to ensnare us. Unavoidable temptations and hang-ups impede our free flight. When we do find ourselves snarled in a negative thought process, we naturally try to free ourselves. But the twisting and fighting can leave us even more caught than before. The way out is not in our own strength and efforts.

When we stretch out our arms to God in a plea for help, His Spirit comes to lift us up out of the branches and intertwined vines. He carries us into clearings in the sky, forcing the vines to fall off. God's Holy Spirit can bring us out of any muddled situation. Above the treetops He can show us His point of view and empower us to take a hawk's flight of freedom, knowing how to dodge the branches and vines that no longer have power to trap us.

God, thank You for Your forgiveness and willingness always to lift me out of any entanglement in my life and bring me into freedom. Amen.

A BIG ROCK

There is none holy like the LORD:
for there is none besides you;
there is no rock like our God.

1 SAMUEL 2:2 ESV

A row of rocks lining the lake are arranged randomly in different sizes and shapes. Some are jagged from erosion. Others are smooth and round. Among the bigger rocks are smaller ones with stones, pebbles, and sand underneath. It's fun to walk from rock to rock, balancing and placing your feet strategically so you can hop to the next.

Common sense tells you to choose the bigger rocks, which are sturdier and roomier. You know from stepping on the smaller ones that they are more likely to shift or tumble. But then you come to one massive rock that's unlike any of the others. It's so big that you have to climb up it in order to sit on top. Its sturdiness assures you it's unmovable and completely secure.

When we choose salvation in God through Jesus, it is like standing on the biggest, sturdiest rock in any lake in the world. It won't shift or tumble no matter the weather of the day. Our God is a Rock that is unmatchable and unchangeable. No other rock is greater, sturdier, or more solid than He. When we climb up this Rock and look out over our lives from His vantage point, we dwell securely.

God, there is no rock like You to hold me up through
life's challenges. You are an adventure to climb, and
the view is always breathtaking. Thank You!

TREE ROOTS

As you received Christ Jesus the Lord, so walk in him, rooted
and built up in him and established in the faith.

COLOSSIANS 2:6–7 ESV

A tree's roots meander over and under the ground in tangled trails, and you follow them like a maze to the trunk. At the base of the tree you find a perfect sitting space, a natural nook, with the exposed roots as arms of the chair and the trunk as its back. Here you take shelter under the leaves, leaning on the ancient, dependable, bark-covered haven.

Under the surface, the tree's roots stretch deep in the ground, absorbing and spreading nutrients and water that strengthen the entire tree to the tips of each leaf. The roots give the tree its vibrant life and a sturdiness to last through the ages, providing shelter and shade for many.

When our roots reach deep in Christ, we grow up into people of faith who are strong for our loved ones when they need someone to lean on. Our character, built by God from the roots up, offers refreshing shade to our friends in a world that can be harsh and unkind. When people sit with us, they feel safe, secure, and nurtured, drawn closer to the heart of God so that their roots can grow deeper too.

God, build me up to be a strong, steady believer who provides
security to people I care about as I take shelter in You. Amen.

CLOUD SHAPES

Now to [God] who is able to do immeasurably more than
all we ask or imagine . . . to him be glory.

EPHESIANS 3:20–21

As children and adults we lie on our backs out in the grass by the lake, looking up into the wide sky. Clouds pass leisurely above and we call out what we imagine the billowing forms look like. One sees a rabbit hopping in slow motion across a clear blue field. Another pictures a pirate ship sailing through calm waters, flag waving in the wind.

The sky is like a blank canvas for us to dream upon, where we might imagine our lives and what heaven is going to be like one day. And no matter how big or wonderful our brains envision these things to be, God is able to do more and make more out of all of our attempts at reaching greatness for His glory.

When we stop to say, "Hey God, what do You think this cloud is?" He may show us plans we never hoped possible. Keep working toward your God-sized goals with open hands and an open mind to what God might do. Clouds shift shapes and locations; let them. Our end goals may look different from what we envisioned, but we can trust the Cloud Maker. Let's leave space in our skies for God to form masterpieces.

God, give me faith to believe You for big things,
and help me to hold these dreams lightly so You
can mold them into Your best plans. Amen.

SPOTLESS

Jesus answered, "Unless I wash you, you have no part with me."

JOHN 13:8

The lawn-green, springy turf with yellow tips of sunlight-spreads out like a play mat under the sprinklers. The metallic spraying contraptions shoot droplets of water in straight lines that reach up to the sky and shower back down. The yard turns into a cascading water park with kids jumping through the showers, yelling and laughing. The mud from the lake washes from their skin as they are soaked and dripping in the cool, refreshing water.

This is what it is like to be washed clean of our sins by Jesus. What a relief it is to go to Him and skip around under His sprinklers. The mud caked on arms and legs, picked up in our imperfect, messy world, is easily drawn off by the droplets of fresh water. But the cleansing goes further: it's as if our souls step into a shower and are scrubbed spotless. We can use our own lakelike, murky water to clean ourselves, but we'll never succeed in being pristine enough for God by our own efforts. Instead, like children, we let Jesus wash us perfectly, for eternity. God's sprinkler system is extraordinary-the water never runs out. He invites us out onto the lawn, dirt and all, for us to run free under His spraying water, cleansing us from the inside out.

Jesus, sometimes I want to try to scrub myself pure before I come to You. Thank You for accepting me in my messiness and inviting me to become spotlessly clean through Your living water. Amen.

MOMENTS OF REFLECTION

I remember the days of old;
I meditate on all that you have done;
I ponder the work of your hands.

PSALM 143:5 ESV

At a lake house, divine pockets of time arise in your day for moments of reflection. You sit in a favorite chair tucked away by a bay window. Sinking into the comfy cushions, you feel the hardy chair arms poised at your sides as if guarding this sacred spot for contemplation. You pick up a journal and pen from the coffee table and gaze through the sheer curtains at the lake beyond. Thoughts surface and then, through your hand, flow onto the page.

Journaling is a therapeutic way to sift through perceptions of recent or past events and reach the deeper conditions of our hearts. We catch meanings and insights we might not have recognized in the moment and savor a second taste of our experiences. When we take the time to meditate on the moments God has given us, we get a clearer picture of the events of our days and how they affect our souls. It is this cherished, fragile part of us that God guards with sturdy arms as we sink into His cushioning embrace and process our days with Him using paper and pen.

God, grant me moments of remembrance and
meditation to journal about the days You've given
me and praise You in the process. Amen.

SUMMERTIME TAG

You are a chosen people . . . God's special possession, that you may declare
the praises of him who called you out of darkness into his wonderful light.

1 PETER 2:9

J ean shorts over swimsuits, sticky watermelon fingers, porch lemonade, and color-wheel umbrellas: these carefree images of summer days light up our minds and push us to break the boundaries, let go, and have fun. By a lakeside bank, cousins and siblings play chase. Every now and then someone yells, "Tag! You're it!" followed by screams, giggles, and the stampede of little feet. Out in the summer sun, this grassy playground is open wide for the children to take up lively games.

I reckon it's been a while since you played a game of tag, but can you recall the thrill of being chased? A friend or family member singles you out and then runs with all his or her might in your direction. For this part of the game, you are chosen out of the crowd as the one he or she is after. It is gratifying to be selected and sought out.

Playing chase is one of God's favorite occupations. He runs after us with all His might. We are the called ones, the objects of His pursuit. When He catches us, we are caught up into His marvelous light, as bright as the summertime where the colors reflect vibrantly off umbrellas, fruit is stickier and sweeter, and there is plenty of space to run around in the freedom found in God's sunny playing field.

God, thank You for always picking me out of the crowd
to pursue me. I love to be caught up in Your light,
brighter than the sunniest summer day. Amen.

FALL TURNINGS

Repent therefore . . . that times of refreshing may come from the presence of the Lord.

ACTS 3:19–20 ESV

When an autumn wind begins to blow through the trees, the breeze's brushstroke colors the leaves one at a time until all at once they are brilliant golds, radish reds, and amber yellows. Although your eyes take in these warm colors, your skin feels the coolness of fall's refreshment. It is a time of turning. Leaves change colors and eventually drift to the ground; all of nature prepares to take a slow turn toward winter.

Autumn presents a season in our spiritual journeys for acknowledging places we have strayed off the path. When we repent, we turn our hearts and minds back to God in fullness for rejuvenation. We hand over what's behind us, our triumphs and our shortcomings, and let the wind of His Spirit blow through and initiate change for the coming seasons. Repentance is meant to bring a fresh breath of life from God's kind heart to us. We are reassured that He has unexpectedly good things ahead to bring out from the fallen, dried-up leaves, which decompose and become fertilizer for growth.

When the leaves put on reds, oranges, and yellows, it is one of the most beautiful seasons of the year, and when we turn to God in everything, we likewise create a pleasing display for earth and heaven. We might even imagine the trees are clapping their hands for us when the autumn wind blows through.

God, turn me back to You in every area of my life. Change in me what needs to fall to make room for the new to come. Amen.

WINTER CHARM

Though the fig tree should not blossom,
nor fruit be on the vines . . .
yet I will rejoice in the LORD;
I will take joy in the God of my salvation.

HABAKKUK 3:17–18 ESV

Barren branches covered in frost stretch out above an iced-over lake. The winter cold seeps down to our bones, locking the joints until we are so chilly that we want to move only if it's toward a fire or the body heat of friends. Frozen winters can be charming, despite the frigidity, with the sparkling frost and a blanket of millions of snowflakes covering the ground in pristine white mounds. Winter also holds romance, with Christmas lights, wonder-felt moments by the fire, and hot cocoa. This romance, or closer companionship with friends and family, warms us and holds us through the cold season.

During wintery times in our lives–when we lose a job or experience a break in a relationship–we can feel as empty and exposed as leafless trees, stripped down of comforts and the things we were holding onto so dearly. To avoid growing cold in these periods, we're always invited to draw near to God and others. God enfolds us, and when we gather close to friends, warmth spreads through us. Then, when we enter seasons of new blessings and fruitfulness again, we will know that closeness to Him and our loved ones is all we really need. Winter months remind us that God is enough, and even in frozen seasons with barren branches, romance and charm can be found in the sweetness of needing Him and our friends and family near.

God, help me to embrace the beauty of needing You and others in barren winter seasons so I will remember what matters most in times of abundance. Amen.

SPRING BREAKTHROUGH

"Behold, I am doing a new thing;
now it springs forth, do you not perceive it?
I will make a way in the wilderness
and rivers in the desert."

ISAIAH 43:19 ESV

Spring means blossoms on every branch, green grounds all around, rainstorm meets rainbow. It's unpredictable, untameable, and groundbreaking. Shoots break out of the earth in all varieties: fresh grass blades, budding flowers, and new oak tree saplings. The weather is chancy. One day it might be sunny, not a cloud in the sky, and then the next, lightning bolts shoot between billowing dark clouds and release a downpour of rain upon the earth. Because of this climate spontaneity, vegetation variations come forth in startling fashion, bursting in brilliant wildflower colors across overgrown forest wildernesses.

When life is particularly fickle, when circumstances are not going the way we imagined, or we are experiencing a personal storm, these are prime conditions in which God can bring forth new and miraculous beginnings. The shaking, breaking ground allows for novel, wonderful gifts to come through and establish themselves in our lives. The rainbows after the rainstorms remind us to hold onto God's promises through uncertainty. We will see His spring faithfulness in the flora and greenery that are on their way through the cracked terrain.

Father, point me to the rainbow in the sky when I'm in
the midst of an uncertain, beautifying season. Amen.

A LESSON FROM THE LAKE BOTTOM

We have this treasure in jars of clay to show that this all-
surpassing power is from God and not from us.

2 CORINTHIANS 4:7

The mushiest mud in all the earth is found at the bottom of a lake. Lake water is a murky, foggy green that hinders you from seeing through to its depths. But you know with certainty that you've reached the ground when your feet sink down into the cool, soft silt.

Out on the lakeshore, the mud is thicker. There might even be clay. Clay is wonderful material that is pliable enough to mold and strong enough to hold its form. A potter can fashion clay into a jar; the clay's role is to remain flexible in the potter's hands. In the end, the jar can hold whatever the potter wishes.

In our case, God is the Potter and our role is to surrender and to remain formable in His expert hands. We don't have to be without backbone in this world, as flimsy and infirm as mud at the bottom of the lake. Instead, when we are like clay, God can use His molds to establish our purpose and to display His power. Let's hold the form God has given us and pour out His loving strength to the world.

God, keep me malleable in Your hands and mold me, like clay,
into a durable container that displays Your glory. Amen.

THE COMEBACK CARD

In all things God works for the good of those who love him,
who have been called according to his purpose.

ROMANS 8:28

After an eventful day, evening time rolls in with the lake's tide as the sun sets. The family gathers on the screened-in back porch, and with nothing else planned, someone pulls out a deck of cards. Families often have favorite card games. They might be Go Fish, Crazy Eights, Spades, or other popular picks. Whichever game is chosen, one of the most entertaining points of the night happens when competitiveness escalates and family members start challenging one another in playful banter.

As the teasing escalates, you remain calm throughout the combative jesting because even though you've been behind most of the game, in your hand you now hold the one card you were saving for the end, like a secret weapon. On your turn, you play it and swing the entire game in your favor. Then you win in a surprise comeback! The rest of the family is shocked into silence, then they erupt in laughter and applause, impressed by your game strategy.

Of all the tricks and setbacks the Enemy throws our way in life, God always has the secret weapon, the winning card that swings destiny in our favor. He is on our side. If a game called for playing partners, He would be on your team the entire time. As you surprised your family with a comeback card on the back porch, God will turn things around when you least expect it. His is always a winning hand.

Jesus, thank You for being on my team and always holding the comeback card that shifts events in my favor. Amen.

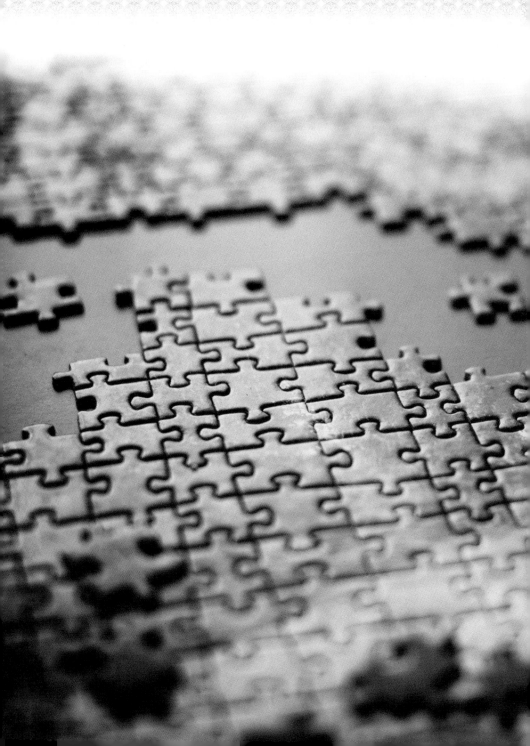

PUZZLE PIECES

"As the heavens are higher than the earth,
so are my ways higher than your ways
and my thoughts than your thoughts."

ISAIAH 55:9

Laid out on a table in the lake-house living space is a partially completed puzzle. Some pieces are spread around and others are gathered in groups of similar colors and patterns. As time passes, people stop throughout the day as if on shifts, to add a piece here and there. The puzzle gradually grows and takes on the form of its intended picture displayed on the box.

Certain parts of the puzzle prove challenging. The puzzle-making team members might grumble that a piece must be missing or that it's never going to get finished. But the key to puzzles is perseverance. At least the team knows what the final picture is supposed to look like, and they will get there together.

Life is a puzzle, and we don't get to see the whole picture to figure out which pieces are supposed to go where. When our lives are crumbled into a bunch of pieces stacked and scattered here and there, seemingly impossible to connect, we can find motivation to press on knowing that God's view is higher than ours. He will connect it all. He holds the box with the big picture displayed.

Father, help me to trust that Your higher view of the puzzle
of my life will bring all the pieces together in time. Amen.

REUNION

*"It is for your good that I am going away. Unless I go away, the
Advocate will not come to you; but if I go, I will send him to you."*

JOHN 16:7

Lake houses are getaway spots in which old friends can reunite away from
everyday life where distance may be the norm. Gathering for a long weekend provides precious time and space to reconnect, tell old stories, reminisce,
and laugh at inside jokes. The lake house becomes an oasis that transports you
all back to times shared. As you refresh the bonds of your friendships, familiar-
ity opens your hearts to each other once again.

When the weekend is over and good-byes have to be shared, it's as if those
unique friends' personalities are close to your heart again and a piece of you
grieves in the parting. But now you have new memories to carry with you until
the next reunion.

When Jesus visited us in human form, He was like a familiar friend we
didn't even know we missed deeply. He ate with us, He joked around, He taught
us truth, He carried our sorrows and shared in our stories. When He left the
earth, He promised it was for the best. He'd send an ever-present Friend, His
Spirit, to be with us always. Distance never has to be the norm between us and
Jesus. He is present at lake-house reunions and back at home in our everyday
lives, keeping us connected through Him.

*Jesus, sometimes I wish You were with me in
human form. Remind me to connect with Your Spirit
whenever I start missing Your presence. Amen.*

DROP ANCHOR

We have this hope as an anchor for the soul, firm and secure.

HEBREWS 6:19

Behind the wheel of a boat, you drive your friends to a lake cove and drop anchor. Because you are sure that it will hold the boat in place, you don't worry about losing this prime location. It's not as if you're hoping for the best—you know your spot is secured.

The word *hope* has a lightness, almost as if it could float like a boat and carry you anywhere the winds of aspiration and desire blow. When we place our hope in things of the world, whether it is a dream job, a new romantic relationship, or acquiring the newest technological gadget, insecurity rises in our hearts because this kind of hope can drift away, out of our reach.

Hope in Christ is of a different sort. It's made of sturdy material, heavy as an anchor. It's a firm foundation as its grip connects us to the unshifting ground of our eternal place in heaven. When we've latched our high expectations to Christ, our boats remain in place, allowing us to keep our spots in the world because we are always fastened to our homes in heaven. Let's turn our boats toward God's kingdom and toss that iron overboard.

Jesus, I want to drop my anchor of hope in You. I love knowing that my spot in heaven is secure! Amen.

YOUR PERFECT ROOM

*"In my Father's house are many rooms. If it were not so, would
I have told you that I go to prepare a place for you?"*

JOHN 14:2 ESV

When I was little, out in our backyard I used to dig a hole in the ground
and place grass inside. Then I would use the dirt to build a little mound
next to it. I'd catch grasshoppers and place them in the grass hole, because obvi-
ously grasshoppers would live in grass. Then I would stand by and wait for ants
to come find the new dirt mound home I'd just built them. It was a masterful
grasshopper/ant duplex! But to my dismay, the grasshoppers would always hop
away and the ants never came. Still, the joy of building a place for the tiny creatures I cared for dazzled my imagination and filled my heart with happiness–so
much that I still remember it more than twenty years later.

God has built a home in heaven for each of us. Thankfully, He is much
better at knowing just what we want or need in our residences. It delights Him
to think of us and prepare rooms better than our imaginations could ever con-
figure. He's gone to all this trouble because we are on His heart and always on
His mind. Although I couldn't draw ants to my dirt mound, God knows how to
beckon us to our homes with Him. My grasshopper guests might have jumped
away, but when we are in our perfect rooms in heaven, we will want to–and we
will get to–stay forever.

*Jesus, thank You for preparing the perfect home
in the Father's kingdom for me. Amen.*

SPIDERWEB REPELLANT

Walk by the Spirit, and you will not gratify the desires of the flesh.

GALATIANS 5:16

Spiderwebs glisten with dewdrops and mesmerize with their intricate patterns. They do us the great favor of catching billions of flies and other insect pests. But sometimes when we're walking through the forest by the lake, they also catch us. A spiderweb stretches across two tree trunks on a path unnoticed until the slender strings wrap around you, making you shiver. The web is strangely sticky, and you keep brushing it off your body for a long time after, never satisfied the web is completely removed.

If you and insects stick so much to the spider's silk, how is it that the spiders don't get caught in their own webs? One of the reasons is that spiders have leg hairs covered with a unique chemical to keep this from happening. The spider's hairs gently touch down on the web when they prance across while the chemical prevents sticking.

Like a spider's web, sin can entangle us, making us feel stuck. It seems impossible to walk through life without greed, lust, envy, selfish ambition, and other vices attaching to us. But when we walk in the Spirit of God, it's as if these pests of the flesh can't hold onto us. God's Holy Spirit acts like a chemical that deactivates the stickiness of sin. We can walk through a spiritual forest empowered, knowing that even the most elaborate webs the Enemy designs can't catch us.

God, You've designed spiders wonderfully to keep them from falling into their own traps. Show me how to walk by your Spirit every day to keep me from sticking to sin. Amen.

BROTHERLY LOVE

Both the one who makes people holy and those who are made holy are of the same family. So Jesus is not ashamed to call them brothers and sisters.

HEBREWS 2:11

Growing up we went to the lake on family vacations, and once there I just wanted to follow my two older brothers around and be part of any game or activity they were playing. If they were swimming, I was dog-paddling around them. If they were playing a board game, I was right there asking about the rules and trying to join. If they jumped off a cliff, I literally followed. (To clarify, the cliff was over deep lake water. My brothers wouldn't lead me into danger.) I'm sure I was a bit of an annoyance when I tagged along, but they looked out for me, and I adored them.

As we grew up, one brother took on the role of caretaker, fixing things for me when they broke, and gift-giver, such as when he won me a stuffed Minnie Mouse at a grabbing machine. The other brother became a sort of spiritual mentor and protector. He helped lead me to Jesus, asked about the health of my heart, and kept any boys with less-than-honorable motives away. But what I loved most about them was their friendship.

Our Friend Jesus protects us, gives us good gifts, and takes care of our hearts. He enjoys our company and includes us in what He is doing in the world. He knows us fully, and His actions toward us are always selfless. Jesus is the best Brother: He loves us so much that He gave His life for us. He was willing to do *anything* to draw us into the family fold. He is never bothered by our following Him around like a tagalong little sister; in fact, He invites us to do so.

Jesus, whatever You are doing, I want to be right there doing it with You. Thank You for being a Brother who is also my Friend. Amen.

PURE RAINBOW

Create in me a pure heart, O God,
and renew a steadfast spirit within me.

PSALM 51:10

A rainbow arches over a lake like a bridge of brilliant parallel colors stretching from one shore to the other. Red melds into orange lined by yellow, grows to green, and transitions to blue with a pink fade. All these colors originate from one source, the white light of the sun. When the light travels through watery prisms, it refracts and reflects and presents a spectrum of colors. These pigments shoot out from the rain like a paint can spraying an arch in the sky.

Purity is holiness in action, shining out from a clean heart made new by God. We often think of purity as following a list of rules about what not to do, think, or say. But as white light is made of all of the colors of a rainbow, purity in our lives with God is meant to be full of all the good, honorable, and colorful aspects of life. The way paint isn't supposed to stay inside a can, this gift is not meant to stay inside us. God presses down on the nozzle and propels it forward to be displayed as vividly as a rainbow arching over a lake.

Father, purify my heart so that when Your light hits
it, I reflect Your colorful character. Amen.

DOWN TO THE ROOTS

He heals the brokenhearted
and binds up their wounds.

PSALM 147:3

The damp land next to the lake offers a treasure hunt for eager children. Kids will spend all day digging and searching for slimy, segmented earthworms coated with the dirt of the earth. When they find one with its head sticking out of the ground, they pull it out, and it stretches like a rubber band until it pops out and recoils. In the kid's palm, it wiggles and squirms as the child prods it gently, delighted with the capture.

We're a little bit like those rubbery invertebrates. When something or someone pulls us out of our cozy emotional places, we also recoil with fear. Perhaps a failure or pain from the past resurfaces. These moments are opportunities to dig deeper into the problem, to the root. Earthworms burrow into and aerate the ground, letting oxygen and water seep through to the roots of plants. It can be uncomfortable digging around the past and letting God touch and prod the tender roots of our lives, but He is creating space for us to breathe, bringing nutrients to decaying parts and refreshing water to heal and form strong roots. Like a treasure hunter, God seeks out the bruised and dirt-ridden parts of us and holds us in His palm as a prized possession to make whole again.

God, when old habits and setbacks resurface,
reach to my roots and bring wholeness to a greater
measure. Make me rich at my core. Amen.

APPLE OF GOD'S EYE

Keep me as the apple of your eye.

PSALM 17:8

Apples are an easy snack to grab when you're heading out of the house and to the water for the day. The hearty, healthy, juice-filled bites are sweet and satisfying whether you munch under a tree or out on a boat. Wherever you sit to enjoy the snack, God watches you cheerfully. In old times, the pupil of the eye was known as the "apple." It's in this black, round center where the objects of our gaze appear. If we could see the eyes of God, we would always find our reflections there.

Being the apple of God's eye means we are cherished ones, chosen and loved by Him. His affections don't change, and His gaze is steady, loving us at all times. He watches over us faithfully, and not only when we are engaged in something important or exciting to witness. He enjoys seeing us in ordinary moments of leisure, even when we're doing something as simple as chewing on an apple. At times when we aren't performing or striving, we are simply ourselves, and in God's view, we are simply enough. When we stop to savor little gifts in life and moments in nature, God smiles and His eyes light up as the objects of His gaze enjoy His creation, under an apple tree or out on a boat.

God, when I'm partaking in something as simple as eating fruit for a snack, remind me that even then You are watching over me as the apple of Your eye. Amen.

MOUNTAIN LION MAMAS

The Lord . . . will roar like a lion.
When he roars, his children
will come trembling from the west.

HOSEA 11:10

At lakes near national parks of the West Coast, every so often someone will spot a mountain lion. These elusive cats are formidable predators with strong jaws and sharp teeth. You don't want to be caught on the wrong side of the sliding glass door when a mountain lion lurks outside. Their muscles make their strikes deadly as they protect their territories and provide for their prides.

A different scene occurs in the den of the mountain lion where the cubs are kept. One brave cub stumbles forward at the return of its mother back with dinner caught fresh. The cub glances up at its mom and rubs affectionately against her jaws, grazing the giant teeth. The cubs trust that their mother is their guardian and protector. She would not use her teeth to harm her cubs.

As our Parent, God has characteristics that can be intimidating. He is strong, fierce, and a warrior for good across the world. Oftentimes in Scripture He is depicted as a lion. This is meant to comfort and encourage us. His roar dispels the Enemy and calls us home, where we can nestle next to His fierce jaws, unafraid. Mountain lions may be difficult to spot, but we can always detect God our Lion next to us in a protective parental stance.

God, give me confidence in Your heart for me so I can draw
near You, knowing that Your strength is my protection. Amen.

HEART HEALTH

Above all else, guard your heart,
for everything you do flows from it.

PROVERBS 4:23

Avocados ripening in a fruit basket on the kitchen counter is a welcome sight in any lake house. Although green and dense, they are in fact not vegetables, but of the fruit family. This versatile ingredient works well with many salads, sandwich fillings, and even some chocolate desserts. There are actually a few adventurous ice cream flavors that feature avocados, or you might find them in a batch of healthier brownies. Whether or not you can get on board this food trend, it is indisputable that avocados are good for your heart. The healthy fat held inside these leather-encased, kiwi-colored ovals lowers cholesterol levels and reduces the risk of heart disease and stroke. Avocados are nature's heart protectors.

Along with our physical hearts, our spiritual hearts need protection too. Our emotions, thoughts, intentions, and actions spring from our hearts and move our whole lives. But the way to guard this most precious part of us is not through building hard encasements around them so they can't ever be touched. Our hearts would suffocate, harden, and cease to beat out life. Instead, allowing the covering of God's love around them, as well as the friendship of dependable, godly people, will help keep our hearts encased and cushioned as though with a layer of healthy fat, ripening in God's basket where they belong.

God, where I have put walls around my heart
to shield myself, gently replace them with the
sheath of Your protective affection. Amen.

WEEPING WILLOWS

We do not know what to pray for as we ought, but the Spirit
himself intercedes for us with groanings too deep for words.

ROMANS 8:26 ESV

Weeping willows bend without breaking. As their branches arch over and touch the grass or water, their light leaves cascade to the ground like streaming tears. There is a softness to their stature, a submissiveness to their countenance. They are lovely and wonderful in their weeping.

We can be beautifully and willingly submissive to the heart of Jesus. Bowing at His feet, we can allow ourselves to be soft and tender toward His desires for the world. This posture may bring tears to our eyes as our hearts break for the pain we witness. But when we pray, Jesus helps us by connecting us to heaven so our intercession ushers His light, love, and hope into these darker places.

In our prayers for the world, we must persist in staying near the Water of Life, where we are replenished and encouraged, always holding an eternal mindset. Willows are planted mainly near streams and lakes because their roots always grow determinedly toward water. When we bend gracefully like a willow tree in prayer, we won't break under the harshness we see in the world because the reality of heaven gives us strength.

God, soften my heart to bend toward the world in prayer,
even if it brings me to weeping. Your eternal love and
perspective will strengthen and uplift me. Amen.

LAKE MIRROR

Now we see in a mirror dimly, but then face to face.

1 Corinthians 13:12 esv

Legs dangling over the end of the dock, you sit looking out over the lake water. There is no breeze, but the sun is dropping behind opaque clouds, cooling the air. It's a soft silver sunset and the lake reflects the slate-tinted sky. The water is still. Leaning over the dock, you can see your reflection as if you were gazing into a mirror.

On this side of eternity, we see glimpses of who God is through His glory displayed in tangible creation. Mountains speak of His majesty. The ever-changing brushstrokes of colors in the sky reveal His limitless palette. Microscopic bacteria holding together the balance of entire ecosystems show the divine detail of our interdependence. And then there are humans, made in His image, each expressing unique pieces of Him. God is a beautiful mystery. Combining all of the diverse aspects of His creation still provides only a shadow of who He is in fullness.

One day we will see Him face-to-face, but for now we can look out over lake waters and know that in the reflected images of ourselves, God's image also appears.

Father, I want to see pictures of who You are demonstrated in nature. When I look at my reflection, I want to see how I am like You. Amen.

GOD THE GARDENER

God arranged the members in the body, each one of them, as he chose.

1 CORINTHIANS 12:18 ESV

Flower beds on a lake-house lawn require care and attention to flourish. They need fresh mulch rich in nutrients, some sunlight, regular watering, and the weeds pulled from around them. The gardener chooses all the flower types and purposefully places them in specific areas in the beds to grow into an arrangement of complementary colors and pleasing patterns. Each pocket of pedals in a group adds to the overall design.

It's fun to walk by gardens and point out your favorite flowers with a friend because chances are, her floral tastes will be different from yours. No single flower is everyone's first preference. In the same way, our unique personalities will be gifts to the people God brings around in life. We shouldn't expect to be everyone's favorite. It is more important that we be ourselves and exhibit the unique qualities God has given us than be liked by everybody.

Each of us is an irreplaceable part of God's garden. If God the Gardener is pleased with us as He prunes, waters, and brings nutrients, we gain a true understanding of who we are, valuing His view of us over others'.

God, I trust that You are growing and pruning me
into a unique and irreplaceable part of Your garden.
Help me to see myself through Your eyes. Amen.

GAZEBO GETAWAY

"When you pray, go into your room and shut the door
and pray to your Father who is in secret."

MATTHEW 6:6 ESV

A gazebo near the lake provides an idyllic getaway spot hidden from the public eye. Its hexagonal shape with open walls holding up a pointed roof looks like part of a castle's tower. Inside the gazebo, you feel safe encased in its sanctuary. It's a somewhat private place for a couple to share time together under the domed peak.

Majority rules that public displays of affection can be uncomfortable for onlookers. But in a secluded place, a sweet kiss or loving words are appropriate and some of the most tender things we can share. Yet the closest relationship we will ever experience in life is with God. He is constantly by our sides and knows every thought, intention of the heart, and detail down to the number of hairs on our heads. He also longs to spend time with just us.

Jesus tells us to get away behind closed doors when we pray to God. Our prayers, when we open our hearts and minds to God, are dear moments to the Father that are just between us and Him. To "perform" prayer out in the open for show steals away the sweetness. Choose a place or two where you can spend time alone with God and enjoy His company and conversation in prayer. Designate your own gazebo getaway spot with the One who knows and loves you best.

Father, point out perfect places in my life where we can draw
away from the public eye and spend time together. Amen.

FLYING ON THE GROUND

Solid food is for the mature, for those who have their powers of discernment trained by constant practice to distinguish good from evil.

HEBREWS 5:14 ESV

Ready, set, go!" A group of children race off on a bike adventure around the neighborhood. The directions they choose are all their own. The training wheels are off, and they control the speed of the wheels and the amount of wind in their faces. The height of a bike ride is cruising down a hill, feet off the pedals, one arm in the air, two if the rider is brave enough. It's like flying while on the ground.

Life can bring us freedom of choice and actions we never thought possible. As we mature we reach new heights of adulthood and responsibility, and we learn to know ourselves, experience God, and discern right from wrong. Our training wheels are off and we have freedom to fly on the ground, trusting God to go ahead of and behind us. Some life choices can seem too big for us, but God is bigger than our plans, and His will is dynamic, spinning together the events and choices of life more quickly than we spin our wheels.

We do have a free and open road before us. The Enemy will try to trip us up with lies, saying we don't have liberty in Christ after all. If we make a wrong turn, he taunts that God will be disappointed and stop blessing us. This is not true. God is the One who took off our training wheels and set us on the bike adventure of a lifetime. If He says we're ready, we're ready. So go!

God, help me to trust that You go before me as I make choices in the freedom of maturing in You. Amen.

HOPE LIKE ADRENALINE

We also glory in our sufferings, because we know that suffering

produces perseverance; perseverance, character; and character, hope.

ROMANS 5:3–4

O n an early morning run by the lake and through trails in the surrounding woodlands, you first set a slower pace. Your joints are still stiff from the night's rest, and your muscles are just warming up. After a mile you still can't shake the stubborn drowsiness and lack of desire to push through. This is when perseverance is paramount. You make the decision to kick it up a notch. This determination brings with it fresh winds of energy, and you finally catch your stride. All of your muscles working now, you feel in control and as if you could carry on for miles on end.

Eventually you reach your goal and bring your pace down to a jog, then a walk. Heading back to the house, you feel your cells buzzing with energy as your brain releases endorphins and they spread through your body. The mental boost of this chemical brings high hopes for the day ahead. We often meet trials and suffering initially with the mind-set that we won't make it, but when we take another step forward, we find new strength and energy to carry us through. Then the unexpected happens: hope courses through us like adrenaline.

It's not a fleeting hope but a strong one that pulses through our core. If your pace seems like slow going at first, press into your stride and remember the natural high of hope is on the way.

God, when I get weary in my "run" with You, help me press
on to get my second wind and the resultant hope. Amen.

BREAD AND BUTTER

We have seen his glory, the glory of the one and only Son,
who came from the Father, full of grace and truth.

Bread machines are a remarkable culinary invention that can revolutionize the routine of a kitchen. The beneficial, if a bit bulky, appliance sits on a counter while baking a sumptuous loaf inside. The preparation is quick and easy. You add water to a premade packet of ingredients for your chosen type of bread and place the dough in the center of the machine. Then you can set the timer to start baking at a specific time during the night so that just as everyone is waking, the bread is rising and wafting its irresistible scents throughout the house.

First to the kitchen, you open the lid to see the rounded-top, rectangular mound that softly receives your touch like warm memory foam as you lift it out. When you cut into it, the scent enveloping you makes you feel as if you're standing in a field of wheat lightly toasting under the sun. Opening the refrigerator, you take out the butter and spread it over an open-faced square of bread. The butter melts as quickly as your mouth is now watering. You take a bite before even sitting down.

Truth and grace go together like bread and butter. Without butter, bread can be dry, lacking flavor. Without bread, butter is flavorful but short of substance, without anything to grab hold of or to enhance. Grace covers us and freely flavors our lives with the richness of heaven, while truth grounds us and strengthens us with substance.

Jesus is the perfect mixture of truth and grace. Instead of going through the impossible task of combining the right amount of both ingredients ourselves, we can embrace Jesus, who measures everything well, and let Him revolutionize our lives.

> *Jesus, help me to enjoy grace and truth as much*
> *as I do bread and butter. I want You to thoroughly*
> *alter my life with Your presence. Amen.*

BOOKS ABOUND

All Scripture is breathed out by God.

2 TIMOTHY 3:16 ESV

It is easy to spot on a bookshelf which volumes are favorites. Their tattered covers, broken-down bindings, and worn, yellowing pages are evidence of the many times we took them off the shelf to sit once more in a cozy reading spot and delve into our beloved literary worlds.

When we read a book, something special happens that is different from what happens when we listen to a story or watch a movie. Printed literature is more intimate. Others can listen to a recording or watch a plot unfold on a film with us, but only one pair of eyes reads a book. You have to make sense of it for yourself and interpret what the narrative is conveying in a personal way. In a sense, the stories and characters become a part of us and have the ability to influence us deeply.

The many varied plots and people of the Bible share this capacity to impact our lives. Scripture abounds with books, anecdotes, and words of wisdom that are more than just impressive prose and poetry providing an escape from everyday life. When we sit down to read the Word of God, something not just special but supernatural happens. The breath of God rises from the pages and enters our spirits, bringing new revelation for the day and transforming us from the inside out. Let's delve into the Bible so often that it is the most worn-out, well-loved book on our bookshelves.

God, thank You for life-giving Scripture. I want to take in every word You've breathed so it can renew and change me. Amen.

TADPOLE GENETICS

We all, with unveiled face, beholding the glory of the Lord, are being transformed into the same image from one degree of glory to another.

2 CORINTHIANS 3:18 ESV

Tadpoles captivate children–and then children capture tadpoles! Under rocks by the bank, the tadpoles swimming and shooting about in all directions create a chaotic scene that delights kids. It's an exciting game to try to reach out fast enough to catch one. Once a tadpole is caught, the kids gather around. When the captor opens his or her hand, revealing the tiny creature, something about the sight surprises the little ones, and they inch closer, peering into their friend's hand in a huddle. They've never caught a tadpole like this one before. It has two minuscule froglike legs!

In metamorphosis, the tadpole is transforming from stage to stage into a frog. It's a natural phenomenon, planted within the tadpole's DNA, that sets the tadpole on a cycle of becoming what it was destined to be.

Likewise, when we meet Christ in a genuine encounter in our lives and make the decision to receive Him as Savior, something miraculous occurs. We begin the process of regeneration as He makes us into new creations. To the very fiber of our beings, His Spirit works in us, transforming us into the likeness of Jesus. Like children marveling over the stages of a tadpole, the angels gather around and marvel at us. Through each step we become more and more the people He destined us to be.

Father, the mystery of becoming who I am in Jesus is amazing. Encourage me in the process with how far I have come in each step taken with You. Amen.

PLAYING FETCH

*Through him then let us continually offer up a sacrifice of praise to
God, that is, the fruit of lips that acknowledge his name.*

HEBREWS 13:15 ESV

On a sunny day you stand on the lakeshore grass, stick in hand, with your beloved dog sitting obediently at your side watching the stick with a tongue-out, wide grin. At the first flick of your wrist he is off, kicking up tufts of grass behind him. Racing to the wooden prize, he runs past it, doubles back, and picks it up in his mouth, looking at you. You clap for him and he runs back to you, drops the stick at your feet, and awaits your congratulatory pats and the highly desired response, "Good dog!" As much as your dog likes the stick, he loves you with all his canine strength.

Imagine if when we played fetch with our dogs, they ran after the stick or ball and then kept running, not even looking back. That would defeat the purpose of the game as well as leave us a bit bruised in heart. When God offers us good gifts, He is happy for us to have them. But if we take them and run off to enjoy them alone, we miss the point.

Instead, we can run back to Him in gratitude, acknowledging the One who gave us the blessing, which strengthens the bond between us and Him. We can drop our "stick" at His feet and hear from Him words of affirmation and encouragement. As delight fills a dog at praise from its master, joy fills us up as God speaks love over us and we sit obediently by His side, ready for another game of fetch.

God, I will receive Your gifts gladly and enjoy them by Your side. Our bond is better than any other blessing. Amen.

A RARE SHELL

"The kingdom of heaven is like a merchant in search of fine pearls, who, on finding one pearl of great value, went and sold all that he had and bought it."

MATTHEW 13:45–46 ESV

Although not nearly as prolific as an ocean, lakes and streams wash shells onto the shore. They are often hidden among rocks and dirt. Children can search for cool stones to collect, but if one discovers a shell, particularly a spiraled one with a unique, wavy pattern, it captures their imaginations along with their hearts.

We could search the whole world over for "rocks" to collect in our lives. Some of us acquire worldly possessions and exciting experiences. These endeavors aren't bad in themselves, but when they start possessing our hearts, when we set our minds on them, we are robbed of the space where Jesus alone belongs. Our hearts' affections become focused on serving ourselves and adding to our belongings and distracted from investing in relationships with our family, friends, and church community.

When we let go of our grasp on worldly gifts, our hearts are released to store up treasures in heaven through investing in relationships, people, and growing the kingdom of God. Collectibles kept in the cache of God–love, joy, peace, faith, trust–are like precious metals that do not tarnish. When we set our desire on them, Jesus keeps our hearts pure and untainted, captivated by His kingdom, like children in awe over an extraordinary shell.

Jesus, guide me to seek after valuables in this life that will last into the next one. Amen.

BANQUET ON A BLANKET

You prepare a table before me
in the presence of my enemies;
you anoint my head with oil;
my cup overflows.

PSALM 23:5 ESV

L akeside picnics are blanket banquets. A provisional display of fruit medleys piled high, sliced meat from the deli, fresh bread and crackers, bowls
of potato or macaroni salad, dessert platters of cookies and brownies, and
coolers of drinks, runs from one side of the blanket to the other. The family
members gather around and fill up their plates to the brim. Children have cookies tumbling off the tops of their full rations. Still, there is always more to go
around.

As delicious as the food tastes, it is the surroundings that bring about
carefree feelings that really allow you to enjoy the picnic. The trees, grass, and
quietly rippling lake waters, plus the clean air and blue skies, lift your spirits as
you feel safe and provided for in this space. You can relax and enjoy.

Out in the world, some will wish us harm, often without reason. From jeal-
ously, bitterness, or plain maliciousness, some want to destroy our God-given
provisions in life or trample on our picnics. But the Bible tells us that even in
the presence of enemies, God prepares a banquet before us. We can relax and
enjoy and trust that He will guard what He has given us, His presence and favor
surrounding us like safe lakeside scenery.

And even if we are stolen from in this life, God's smorgasbord up in heaven
is always ready to replenish our feasts.

Father, help me to enjoy whatever You provide in security because I know You are the Host of the picnic. Amen.

MARMOT IN A MEADOW

Those who hope in the LORD
will renew their strength.
They will soar on wings like eagles;
they will run and not grow weary,
they will walk and not be faint.

ISAIAH 40:31

On a mountain hike you climb around a corner, unaware that a furry, log-shaped critter with beady eyes and black nose up in the air is sniffing your scent as you draw near. You walk around the bend and catch a glance of the little mammal on top of its rock-pile lookout before it scurries away. Was that a groundhog? Its tan underside and mountainous home mean it's actually a yellow-bellied marmot. If you want another view of the marmot, climb up to a high-elevation meadow where you will likely find one basking in the sun on a boulder, nibbling on a flower.

The majority of our lives are spent here on mountain meadows where life is level and ordinary, in between the mountains and valleys. When we first start our journey with Jesus it's exciting and new and we feel as if we are soaring over mountaintops like eagles. Then when we touch back down, we may run into lowlands of challenge and testing. When we walk out onto a meadow, life slows and we discover God's peace and presence in the field, giving us strength and the ability to continue faithfully with Him. There will be seasons of the mountains and valleys again, but for now we can lie out on a boulder like a marmot and bask in the steadfast love of God.

Father, lead me to the meadows where I can be established in my faith and recharged for the journey forward. Amen.

FLOWER CROWNS AND STICK SWORDS

You shall be a crown of beauty
in the hand of the LORD,
and a royal diadem in the hand of your God.

ISAIAH 62:3 ESV

A circle of young girls, sitting on the grass cross-legged, pick little white-flowered weeds. Then they knot them together and connect the ends to each other. The result is a delicate flower crown they drape lightly on their heads, transforming them into princesses.

On a grassy knoll to the right of the girls, a band of boys strike at one another with sticks in a game of make-believe swordplay. The daring adventures in their minds upgrade them to prince status. Even though the girls' crowns are made of meager weeds and the boys' blades of breakable wood, it's the noble glow created inside that makes them feel like royalty.

When was the last time we felt our hearts beam from the knowledge that we are princesses or princes? It seems frivolous and immature to think of ourselves in that way now. As we grow out of childishness and into independence and self-sufficiency, we might believe we have given up our right to be adored, honored, and cherished like royalty. But our heavenly Father always sees us as His children, and He is King. He builds and guides our characters as we mature, but in His eyes we never lose the ability to make His heart grow warm and tender when we turn our faces toward Him in trust and dependence. He is fashioning for each of us a crown in heaven that will never wither the way even the most gorgeous flower crowns will on earth.

*Father, thank You for adoring and cherishing me
no matter how old I grow. I never want to be too
"mature" to enjoy Your royal affections. Amen.*

CAMP CHAIR PREPARED

Put on then, as God's chosen ones, holy and beloved, compassionate
hearts, kindness, humility, meekness, and patience.

COLOSSIANS 3:12 ESV

Carrying a long narrow bag strapped over one shoulder, you head out to enjoy lakeside time in the sun. At the shore, you swing the bag around in front of you and pull out the folded-up camp chair. You extend the legs, it pops open, and you settle in. The bottom and back dip just right to support your back, and the arms are at the perfect height to rest your elbows. A few clouds in the sky promise incremental shade, and your view is just level with the horizon, giving you the perfect angle to take in the natural scene. You have never felt more prepared for a day by the lake.

What we carry into our days affects how ready we are to interact with others and handle challenging situations. God gives us directions to tote along compassion, kindness, humility, meekness, and patience. If we leave them at home, our "seats" may be hard and splintered, giving us cause for irritability. Slinging godly virtues over our shoulders for the day sets us up for comfort so we can respond to circumstances gracefully. Let's have the foresight to pack our morning bags with the attributes of God. Then we'll be ready for whatever comes into view.

God, before I walk out the door in the mornings,
remind me to equip myself with Your attributes so I
can handle my day with godly reflexes. Amen.

BLESSINGS VERSUS LUCK

"The LORD bless you and keep you;
the LORD make his face shine on you."

As you're sitting underneath a great oak, light flickers through the leaves in the shade and warm air carries from the lake and circles around you. The book you've been reading now rests at your side, and you are lost in thought. A rabbit hops around the large tree trunk, waking you from your reverie, and is unstartled by your calm presence. You purposely remain still in hopes of keeping the furry friend around. Still in a pensive state, you wonder why anyone ever thought that a rabbit's foot was lucky.

We look to luck because we strongly desire that life goes well. Success seems often out of our grasp or to happen only to the chosen few. Deep down we know it's nonsense, but we can't help but feel a sort of comfort from a lucky charm, or a routine we believe in some small way tilts fate to our side.

The truth is, we have the favor of God freely given to His children. His face toward us, His light upon our paths, and His love and guidance are all we need to know that He can work things to go well for us in life. We can let go of misplaced faith in good fortune, enjoy moments of reverie, and trust in the God who created the rabbit's foot and controls our destinies.

Father, I trade the solace I sometimes find
in trinkets and routines for trusting in Your
favor and the light of Your face. Amen.

WATERCOLOR LIFE

In their hearts humans plan their course,
but the LORD establishes their steps.

PROVERBS 16:9

D own by the lake in a grassy area of land protruding into the water, you sit on a blanket with a watercolor kit, cup of water, brushes, and sketchbook positioned around you. You dip a brush into the water, then swish it around the blue square of paint, transfer the color to the palette, and then repeat with green and the other colors, mixing the paints and preparing mimics of the colors you see. Moving your brush over the paper now, you make each stroke with purpose and direction. At the same time, you allow the water to spread and travel wherever it will.

In order to embrace the art of watercolor, we have to be willing to give up some control. Our mixing of the paint and placement of the brush across the paper will profoundly affect the picture, but the water transforms it into a moving, living image. Our decisions and chosen steps forward affect the forming depiction of our lives. When we place our plans before God, His water spreads where it will from our strokes. This partnership with Him carries the artwork to new depths of texture and blending of pigments. Take out your painting tools and make your brushstrokes with confidence, and watch God transform your life into a watercolor masterpiece.

Father, teach me to make bold brushstrokes in life, allowing Your
Spirit to shape the end result into a beautiful piece of art. Amen.

THE DIMENSIONS OF LOVE

How wide and long and high and deep is the love of Christ.

EPHESIANS 3:18

Lakes can be massive. You can stand at the edge and look out to the right and left, straining your eyes, and not see either end. Out in the center their depths can be unreachable by the deepest dive from the highest point on a boat. Even riding on a boat, you can feel as if the turns and coves are unending.

Lakes do, however, have an end and a beginning. They provide spacious water worlds where you can spend days adventuring and exploring and never get bored. Eventually you could map out each cove and corner and learn all the turns and hidden places.

Similarly, the love of God is deeper than the deepest lake and more far-reaching than the longest waterways. Our relationship with God is an adventure that never runs out of new coves and turns that teach us new lessons and show us layers of who He is. The more we know and grasp, the more we realize there is more to explore.

The lake has boundaries at the sky and corners of land, but the dimensions of God's love go on in every direction and never cease. You can strain your heart and mind to try to grasp it, but until you jump in and explore, you won't fathom just how deep, wide, high, and long the love of God is in Christ.

God, I want to jump in and explore for myself the
far reaches of the love You have for me. Amen.

FOLLOWING IN JESUS' WAKE

Peter said . . . , "See, we have left everything and followed you."

MATTHEW 19:27 ESV

Sprawled out on top of a giant tube so full of air it swells under your arms, you grasp two handles at the top. You hear the rumbling start of a motor and within seconds, the rope in front of your tube tightens as it pulls you forward with the speedboat. Accelerating, the boat cuts effortlessly through the water and you soar on the wake in the back, wind whipping your hair, hands grasping the rope, and heart pounding. This is what it feels like to leave everything behind and go forward wholeheartedly, all-in.

Wherever the boat travels, you go with it. If the boat makes a sudden turn, you go flying and hopping across the water. When we leave everything behind and follow Jesus, we ride on top of the wake behind Him. Wherever Jesus goes the miraculous follows and life bubbles up around Him as the kingdom moves forward. As followers, we are connected to Him like the rope to the tube. Hang on tight and get ready for a fantastic ride advancing the kingdom with Jesus at the lead.

*Jesus, wherever Your kingdom is advancing, pull
me along for the ride of a lifetime. Amen.*

STORING ACORNS

"While they were going to buy [oil], the bridegroom came, and those who were ready went in with him to the marriage feast, and the door was shut."

MATTHEW 25:10 ESV

Walking in the backyard of the lake house toward the trees, you sit on a wooden bench by the creek. Near your feet, a squirrel is inching toward you, a few steps at a time, stopping to eye you with each movement forward. It looks from your face to your feet, breathing fast and looking determined. Following its line of sight to the ground, you notice an acorn by your right foot. Kindly, you nudge the acorn toward the squirrel who grabs it, stuffs it in its cheek, and scurries off with its prize.

Squirrels gather acorns to prepare for the winter months. Likewise, Jesus tells us to store up "oil" in our "lamps" to be prepared for His return. The oil keeps our flame, or passion and devotion, for Him alive. Although we don't know exactly when He will come back, like squirrels storing up acorns, we know His next appearance is inevitable: Jesus' return is as certain as the changing of seasons.

There are stretches in life when days are normal and nothing significant seems to be going wrong, such as when we are leisurely sitting on a bench by a stream. Even in these times, we are to remain prepared for the Bridegroom, with oil in our lamps–fervent love ablaze, as dedicated as a squirrel after an acorn.

Jesus, when things go well for me and routines
unfold normally, remind me then more than ever
to be ready for Your certain return. Amen.

ROLY-POLY ARMOR

Put on the full armor of God.

EPHESIANS 6:11

A child walks to the bottom of the steps of a front porch, where she sees a flat rock and crouches down to lift it up. Underneath, the dirt is damp and cool, and tiny, oblong insects dressed in grey armor crawl around. It's a colony of roly polies! She picks one up, and it coils into a protective little ball on her palm.

The outer coating of the roly poly is its armor. When it rolls up, all of its softer, more vulnerable areas are safeguarded. God's Word exhorts us to put on the full armor of God to protect ourselves against the Enemy. God has thought of every piece of armor we need to protect vulnerable, valuable parts of us. We are given the "belt of truth" to place around our waists, the "breastplate of righteousness" to cover our chests, "the gospel of peace" to protect our feet, and the "shield of faith" to deflect the Enemy's arrows (Ephesians 6:14–16).

Every morning we can practice putting on each part of the armor of God. We don't have to hide under a rock like a roly poly; we can face each day with confidence knowing that we are covered.

God, prepare me for each day with the armor of truth,
righteousness, peace, and faith so that I advance bravely. Amen.

GRACE AS SUNSCREEN

I pray that the eyes of your heart may be enlightened.

EPHESIANS 1:18

The sun is brilliantly bright. It beams down on us from the sky like a fire-fueled lamp. It wraps us in warmth, and by its light we can see the world around us. Yet we are told that if we stare directly at it for too long, it will blind us. And when we go out for a hot day on the lake, we have to lather up with sunscreen to protect us from its more harmful rays.

Scripture depicts God as "light; in him there is no darkness at all" (1 John 1:5). But His luminous rays are not the kind that scorch. When the eyes of our hearts gaze upon God, the Lord's grace coats our hearts with a sort of sunscreen. We are not blinded or burned, but enlightened. Through His shining we see everything more clearly. Our hearts can be gripped by the radiant glory and beauty of Jesus, and we never have to look away even though He is brighter than a sun ray.

Jesus, cover my heart with Your grace so I can gaze upon Your glory and beauty forever. Amen.

FLAGS OF IDENTITY

Moses built an altar and called it The LORD is my Banner.

EXODUS 17:15

Some lake-house residents practice the charming tradition of mounting decorative flags, which they change every season, on their front porches. During the spring, the house's banner might reflect flowers or an Easter bunny. In the fall, it might sport a cornucopia or medley of autumn leaves. Whether it's winter, spring, summer, or fall, we like to artistically display our favorite aspects of each season's identity to the rest of the neighborhood.

Our clothes, jobs, hobbies, friends, and other preferences can become banners over our lives describing what we enjoy. We may go too far and get offended if someone criticizes one of our favorites. At those times we need to peel back these surface-level aspects of our identity and realize that they are not the core of who we are. We are the Lord's, "fearfully and wonderfully made" by Him (Psalm 139:14).

When the banner over us is the Lord, the other characteristics are still present. It's okay to express our unique gifts, talents, and tastes, but the most important aspect of us is that as believers we represent and display the same banner of Jesus the Savior. Let's mount our flags of identity on the front porch of our lives for everyone to see: we are children of God.

God, thank You for being a banner over my life.
I want my unique qualities and preferences to
decorate a flag that represents You. Amen.

CONSTELLATION CONNECTIONS

The LORD will work out his plans for my life—
for your faithful love, O LORD, endures forever.

L ying on your back in the grass with a couple of friends, you survey a diamond-studded, black velvet sky. As you search the star patterns, you call out common constellations: "There's the Big Dipper!" your friend says. "And that's the Little Dipper under it," another adds. "Oh, there's my favorite, Orion's Belt!" you say, pointing up at the three consecutive stars in a straight line.

Connecting the dots in the sky to create pictures of things like Pegasus or a lion comes naturally to us. We like patterns and purpose and making sense out of seemingly random alignments. Some people even like to look to the stars to make sense out of their lives. They search for their destinies written within the mysterious expanse of galaxies. But lots of it is just space dust.

Our destinies rest in the hands of God. He alone can view our lives from a distance farther than the moon and know where and how to connect the dots. Often the friends next to us in life are included in our life constellations. God's purposes and plans for our lives are not drawn out separately from others'. We can sit with our friends and look at our interwoven lives from a distance and wonder at the astonishing way God connects us and weaves our stories together in a glorious design just like the Milky Way.

Father, help me to see how You are connecting my
story with others' for Your greater glory. Amen.

WHERE THE SKY MEETS THE GROUND

"The kingdom of heaven has come near."

MATTHEW 3:2

The best back porches come with a view. There are trees, maybe a pond, and (hopefully) acres of green grass that stretch all the way to where the sky meets the ground. At this point, the line of the horizon is drawn: the bottom is green, the top is blue. When children draw pictures of nature, they often start by sketching a line separating earth and sky. When children hear Bible stories, they naturally picture heaven and earth in this way, as if a firm line stands between the two.

If you think about the grass and sky in three dimensions, actually, the sky is made up of air, which covers and spreads over the ground, breathing on the grass, in between every blade. The relationship between heaven and earth is more like this three-dimensional visual than the two-dimensional drawing. Heaven has come near, advancing over the ground, breathing on creation.

We can ask Jesus to give us a back-porch view of heaven. Where we draw lines separating heaven and earth, He erases them so that heaven pours out over the earth and into our lives.

Jesus, give me a back-porch view of how heaven and earth relate to one another and to me. Show me where the kingdom is entering. Amen.

SKI TRICKS

*Yet among the mature we do impart wisdom. . . . We impart a secret and
hidden wisdom of God, which God decreed before the ages for our glory.*

1 CORINTHIANS 2:6–7 ESV

Waterskiing is a challenging sport to master. When you watch seasoned skiers, they make it look easy, as if the boat is a smooth-running rocket on the water and the skiers just gracefully hang on for the ride. But when you are first learning to water-ski, finding your strength and balance to avoid falling flat on your face takes a while. Countless practice runs later, you finally get the rhythm down for standing up on the water.

Mature skiers have practiced and trained to be able to control their bodies on the skis and do flips, jumps, and spins. In the changing conditions on the water, they know which way to lean and how to balance and push off in order to land the desired trick. In a similar way we can train our minds, hearts, and bodies in godly wisdom so that even with shifting circumstances, our movements are guided by discernment and poise. We know which ways to lean and jump on the changing events to reach our goals with wise, godly results.

When we first learn to walk in godly wisdom, we might find it just as challenging as waterskiing is to a beginner. We might fall more times than we succeed, but we keep trying and practicing. Eventually we will reach the mature level of manageable flips and graceful jumps, all the tricks of the experts on skis.

*Jesus, help me to reach maturity by using
wisdom until I am "expert" at it. Amen.*

MUFFIN MUNCHERS

Godliness with contentment is great gain, for we brought nothing
into the world, and we cannot take anything out of the world.

1 Timothy 6:6–7 esv

Picture a wooden basket on a kitchen counter containing blueberry muffins blanketed by a checkered cloth: Isn't this a picture of comfort? The cloth keeps the muffins fresh for hungry passersby needing a treat to tide them over till the next meal. These fluffy clouds of cake with bursts of blueberries in each bite are sweet enough to be a dessert, yet light enough to be a satisfying snack that doesn't spoil your appetite for mealtime . . . that is, unless you indulge in one too many.

Our spirits are always hungry and seeking fulfillment. If we don't get our fill from God, we might start stuffing ourselves with too many "snacks," whether they're food, luxury, or entertainment. We overindulge because we feel as though we can't get enough or that the provision won't last, so we have to consume in excess.

In the moments we want to overdo, whatever the source of pleasure, we can turn to God. Nothing fills our emptiness like godliness. Accepting with humility the good gifts of God grows in us a contentment and certainty that we will always be fed and have enough. We can practice the self-control to eat just one of those muffins because we know the next meal will always be provided.

Father, help me believe in Your future goodness
and provision so I don't overconsume what is
available now. Grant me contentment. Amen.

FISH OUT OF WATER

"As the Father has loved me, so have I loved you. Now remain in my love."

John 15:9

F ish breathe by filtering oxygen out of water as it moves through their gills. If a freshwater fish is not immersed in a lake, tank, or river, its breathing mechanism cannot function. Besides oxygen, fish also need food to survive, and unfortunately for them, they often mistake our bait for a meal and are caught up from the water.

Sitting on a dock, you reel in your first catch of the day. As soon as the fish breaks the surface of the water, it flips and wiggles, uncomfortable out of its natural aquatic habitat. The line draws closer to you and you catch the fish swinging in the air. Holding its cool, slick body, you unhook it and hold it steady with both hands. Its eyes are wide, unfamiliar with this dry sensation of air, and it takes little gasps. Because it's so small, within moments you throw the fish back into the water, and it swims off, splashing its tail.

The outside world can bait us with appetizing meals of luxury, fame, and pride that look real but are actually empty of nutrition or sustenance. When we feel uncomfortable or unlike ourselves, like fish out of water, we may realize something has caught our attention and dragged us from abiding in God's love. The good news is that we can always jump back into His waters, where we can never outstay our welcome. God's love rushes over our souls, and we filter out the very breath we need to live. Our hearts do not have specialized gills for surviving outside of His love. Stay drenched and breathe it in.

God, help me be aware of signs that I am no longer abiding in Your love so I can jump back into Your waters and breathe where I belong. Amen.

NAP IN GRACE

*It is by grace you have been saved, through faith—and
this is not from yourselves, it is the gift of God.*

EPHESIANS 2:8

A daybed with white linen sheets or a couch with a light summer blanket at the lake house is a resplendent refuge for a midday nap. The curtains are closed, and you curl up on the bed under the light, cushiony covering. Your head sinks down into the pillow and you breathe in its fresh, crisp case. Perhaps a furry friend joins you. Your thoughts start to slow and your body relaxes, each muscle loosening its grip and giving way to the mattress's comforting hold.

Naps are pleasant and refreshing. When our muscles stop working and relax, they get the rest they need to function smoothly. Grace works in a similar way–it's like taking a nap for your soul. Grace has been given to us as a gift in full measure. Our own efforts to make ourselves fit for heaven and good enough for God are futile and tiring. We have to start with a nap, soaking in God's grace. This means relaxing in our own attempts at working for salvation. It sounds too good to be true that God's grace could be enough, but it is. We can find rest for our souls and hide away for a midday nap in God's grace. When we arise, we are prepared to exercise our moral muscles in godly activities.

*Father, when I start trying to gain Your acceptance
through my own efforts and tire myself out, draw
me away for a nap in Your grace. Amen.*

LIFE PRESERVER

If you declare with your mouth, "Jesus is Lord," and believe in your heart that God raised him from the dead, you will be saved.

ROMANS 10:9

A thick wooden column standing in the water with a rusty hook near the top holds a red ring with four equidistant white stripes and a coiled, long white rope. This life preserver looks idyllic in the lake scenery: the red is lightly fading and contrasts with the teal water and light blue sky. But it does more than look good: a floatation device by the lake is a saving security. We can enjoy the picturesque display, but gazing at and admiring it will not save us if we are caught out in the water in trouble.

People, Christian or not, admire Jesus for His godliness and the light that issued forth from His person. We recognize Him as a good person even if we haven't accepted Him as God and man. His humility, like a fading red life preserver, looks lovely contrasted with the self-seeking landscape of our world. But His kindness and the beauty of His heart are meant to draw us to repentance and salvation. In order for His saving strength to work, we must confess with our mouths and believe on Him in our hearts. Then, no matter where we are out in the water, we continually have this "floatation device" with us. Let's make sure we don't merely revere our life preserver but take it off the column's hook.

Jesus, I love to gaze upon Your beauty in this selfish world. I confess You as Lord and believe in You in my heart. Amen.

MOONBEAMS

"Let your light shine before others, so that they may see your good
works and give glory to your Father who is in heaven."

MATTHEW 5:16 ESV

On a clear evening, the moon shines like a beacon. Without the competition of streetlights, its luminous globe blazes like a flashlight with freshly replaced batteries. But the light is not its own; the moon borrows its radiance from the sun. As the moon orbits the earth, it reflects the sun and sends its beams to every part during the dark hours.

As believers, we live in this space between the earth and the sun. The sun, or light source, is God, and we are not yet in heaven with Him, nor are we called to make earth our permanent home. Instead we travel the world, all of us in our given orbits, doing the good works of God–serving the poor, taking care of the environment, healing the sick, and spreading the message of the gospel. As we let our moonbeams bring light to the world, they point people to the true Source, our Father in heaven. We are His beacons in the night.

God, make my moonbeams bright wherever I travel in Your
world so that people will be drawn to Your brightness. Amen.

TRAVELING IN HARMONY

Live in such harmony with one another, in accord with Christ Jesus, that together
you may with one voice glorify the God and Father of our Lord Jesus Christ.

Deciding to travel on the water with a friend, the two of you carry the boat above your heads and start out in step with one another. Holding the vessel steady and keeping pace, you travel down the grassy slope that leads to the shore. Once the canoe is in the water, the two of you climb in, paddles in hand. Kicking off, you start the easygoing journey paddling on opposite sides. The synchronized work steadily carries the canoe forward. Water laps around the boat in subtle waves, and the lakeside view travels by like a nature film in slow motion.

Unity and cooperation in a peaceful canoe ride are effortless if you both know how to steer. If you decide to turn to the right, for instance, both paddles switch to the left. The key is communication and paying attention to the other's paddling. When we live out life with our friends, it's not as simple to remain on the same page. We have different schedules, unique dreams, and varying interests. If we are intentional about keeping up with one another and pay attention to the others' ups and downs, we know how to pray for our friends and encourage each other in getting to our destinations. Although our gifts and callings are unique, we share in each other's lives, as if we're in the same canoe, paddling forward for God's glory.

Jesus, be the canoe that carries my friends and me forward
in harmony as we paddle toward Your glory. Amen.

BEACH PARADISE

"I have come that they may have life, and have it to the full."

John 10:10

Many lakes have beach areas with sand on the shore and swimming areas designated by buoys or rope. You often see there what you would spot at any ocean beach across the coasts: parents set up umbrellas in the sand, teenagers sunbathe, kids swim with floaties out in the water and build sand castles on the shore. All that's missing are some palm trees, or you might imagine yourself in the Caribbean.

After an entire day in this paradise spot on the lakeshore, you come in sunsoaked. Inside, the heat radiates from your skin, drawn out by the cool air. You feel wonderfully drained. Not only are you tanned, but the sun's rays seem to be glowing in you. You spent your day in the fullest beach experience the lake could offer, and now you are emanating life, joy, and happiness.

When we spend our lives with others using all our energy, not holding back on the adventures of the day, the sun giving us its energy and light the way God in heaven pours into us the light of life to pour out, Jesus grants us life abundant. It's like taking an ordinary beach on a lake and transforming it into an island paradise.

God, send me out in the day to embrace adventure and fun with friends and family. Turn my ordinary days into full days on the beach soaking up Your light. Amen.

ROBIN'S EGG BLUE

He was in the beginning with God. All things were made through
him, and without him was not any thing made that was made.

JOHN 1:2–3 ESV

O n a desk in the lake house a classic ninety-six-piece Crayola set sits open. Each crayon inside is pointed from the use of the sharpener on the back of the box, ready for the first strike of inspiration to color. Among the orange-yellow, navy blue, and tickle me pink, a color with one of the most interesting names holds its place: robin's egg blue. The subtle tones of turquoise mixed in light blue paired with imaginings of tiny eggs inside a robin's nest delight young impressionable minds quick to wonder at any allusion to God's natural world.

Nature inspires our nomenclature, our crafting, and our creativity. We decorate our homes with artwork depicting inspirational nature scenes. We sew stuffed animals for children and tell stories personifying critters and plants, giving them personalities and character. Poetry turns the sun and moon into expressions of love and romance. Flying birds and insects dare us to dream of our own planes of flight.

God has been creating since the beginning, and He placed the same inventiveness in each of us. The way He delights in the robin's work of mending many twigs into a nest for its chicks, He delights in our crafts, from sewing buttons to building rocket ships. Let's take the time to come up with our own "robin's egg blue," or ways of portraying God's creation.

Father, help me set aside time to use my "crayons"—to pursue the unique creativity You placed in me. I want You to marvel at what I make. Amen.

WATERMELON SMILES

"Listen, listen to me, and eat what is good,
and you will delight in the richest of fare."

Isaiah 55:2

Sitting on the front porch of the lake house, you and a couple of close friends hold watermelon slices so big you have to grip them with both hands. At the same time you take bites of the delicious pink iciness. As you eat the rest, juice dribbles down your chins and you look up to laugh at each other's sticky beards. Holding up the rinds to your mouths like smiles, you gather for a picture to share with friends and family at home. The watermelon-smile selfies are posted on social media and in moments followers see the joy in the photos and start craving watermelon themselves.

God invites us to come freely to Him for wholesome, delicious, and healthy food. We can apply this to the earthly meals we consume as well as to the food we feed our souls. While watermelon is a wonderful food for the body, the best soul food is friendship. When we partake of God's goodness by investing in Jesus-centered relationships, we experience some of the sweetest moments life has to offer, like watermelon smiles and laughter on the porch with friends.

God, help me fully enjoy the good gifts You give me, such as friendship and watermelon by a lake on a sunny day. Amen.

DIVING INTO DECISIONS

Let your reasonableness be known to everyone. The Lord is at hand.

PHILIPPIANS 4:5 ESV

You stand at the end of a dock with your hands stretched out over your head, side by side. You bend your knees and leap, arcing over the water. In the dive your hands hit the water first, your head follows shortly after, and then the rest of your body submerges, leaving a splash behind you.

Our days are full of decisions, and the significant ones that seem to determine the direction of our future can feel as frightening as a dive into a lake of undetermined depth. When we face decisions in life, the Lord is at hand. He goes before us, like our hands, hitting the water first, preparing the way.

When we follow God forward in our choices, we are called to walk by faith and not by sight. So even if we can't see the bottom of the lake, we still jump. This kind of faith may seem detached from reason, but we don't leave our minds behind when we leap. Rather our minds become immersed in faith and God is at hand, ready to show Himself faithful. Belief that God will be with us as we move forward in our big plans is what gives us the courage to dive at all.

Father, when I make decisions I want to dive
headfirst into faith in You. Amen.

FIRST-AID KIT

He heals the brokenhearted
and binds up their wounds.

PSALM 147:3

A first-aid kit kept in a lake-house cabinet may contain many different doctoring items, such as Band-Aids, ointments, gauze, tape, pain relievers, and a thermometer, depending on the box. The kit has remedies for all different types of wounds and ailments. With all the outside play, splintered wood, jagged rocks, and other debris hidden at lake bottoms, children particularly will have accidents. This is why we have such kits at hand, for mothers and fathers to tend hurts.

In an imperfect world, we are bound to experience different types of wounds and pains, many times from the people closest to us. It is vital that we take these internal cuts and bruises to God, who won't scold us but will bind up our wounds. He wants our hearts healthy and whole. If not treated properly, "cuts" may become infected, and we risk growing bitter toward others and end up causing the same injuries to our loved ones.

As soon as an injury occurs, whether in our hearts, minds, emotions, or souls–many times all four–we can go immediately to God, whose first-aid kit holds all the remedies to any kind of ache.

God, heal me when I've been hurt by people I trust and love. Help
me to love others well and experience wholeness of heart. Amen.

SPRING SALAD

"Come to me, all who labor and are heavy laden, and I will give you rest."

MATTHEW 11:28 ESV

After a long morning of a strenuous undertaking like yard work, car washing, or a carpentry project, you come into the cool kitchen craving a light lunch. Salads can be fun and nutritious. With the right ingredients, they are filling without weighing you down. Spinach with strawberries, almonds, and blue cheese or mixed greens with apples, pecans, and cranberries: place handfuls of whichever ingredients you choose in a large metal bowl, drizzle on a flavorful dressing, and toss. Your salad provides pure energy to spring your steps forward into the rest of the day.

Hard work is a gift from God, and it requires a lot of vigor. Sometimes we get too preoccupied with our many responsibilities that pile up and weigh us down. When we come to Jesus with our schedules and planners, He reveals to us the activities worthy of our time and efforts–and He may even encourage us to pull back in some places. When we reduce commitments to make room for Jesus, He fills our lives with good gifts, endeavors, and activities.

Then after a laborious day in the yard, in the office, or at home, we come to Him with hungry hearts and His presence is easy to carry, like a light meal. It gives our souls stamina, allowing us to bounce back into the rest of our day.

Jesus, when I pause for lunch, give me wisdom about the activities I choose to occupy my days. Help me choose what's necessary to make room for You. Amen.

TIPTOES

Let us then with confidence draw near to the throne of grace.

HEBREWS 4:16 ESV

All the lights are off in the cabin. It's the middle of the night, and down one hallway the soft steps of a tiptoeing child reach the ears of sleeping parents. The sound is as familiar as an alarm clock and automatically wakes the mother. The bedroom door creaks open and a beseeching little face peeks around the door. Smiling, the mom waves her in. The kid shuffles across the floor and crawls in the bed, snuggling between the two parents. Whether it was a bad dream or loneliness in the darkness, whatever woke the child is soon forgotten and little snores ensue.

God recognizes the sound of His children coming to Him. Even if we are a bit unsure and timid, tiptoeing our way toward Him, He hears us and smiles. Whether it's a disappointed dream that drew us away from Him or the darkness around us, whatever attracts us to seek God He is there and ready to bring us in close. The sounds of our steps always reach His ears.

*Father, whether I'm running or tiptoeing, thank
You for always welcoming me. Amen.*

MIDNIGHT SNACK

Because of his great love for us, God, who is rich in mercy, made us alive with Christ.

EPHESIANS 2:4–5

Sometimes only two to three hours have passed in sleep when your rumbling stomach wakes you. At once pictures of Grandmother's leftover double-layered chocolate cake fill your vision. Before you know it, you're in the kitchen lifting the glass dome of the cake stand and cutting a piece. Sitting at the counter, you sigh as the first forkful melts in your mouth and makes your taste buds chocolate rich.

Because this midnight snack is out of the routine, it is all the more pleasant and deeply enjoyed. When we wake up at random in the middle of the night or have trouble focusing during the day, we may be receiving a nudge from God to take a moment to connect and talk with Him. These moments can be some of the sweetest because they are unplanned. Our minds are relatively silent for once, and our spirits are more open to hear God's tender encouragements. Guard down, we are receptive to His affection.

Take these midnight moments or daydreaming opportunities to reach out to God. They'll fill you even more than Grandmother's cake!

Jesus, make me aware of Your nudges in the night and slow times of my day to turn and receive love from You. Amen.

FOLLOW THE LEADER

Do not conform to the pattern of this world, but be
transformed by the renewing of your mind.

ROMANS 12:2

Around the end of a dock a mother mallard swims into view. Then a tiny yellow-brown ball of fluff paddles right behind her. This duckling surprise is followed by another and then another, until one at a time the cuteness parade ends with a duckling caboose. The miniature mimics of the mother follow her in a cloud of fuzzy bodies and little bills.

When we follow Jesus, we not only go wherever He goes, we look like Him too. Beyond the physical image, our hearts and souls become more like His as we follow our Leader. We love the way He loves, forgive our friends for wrongdoing, pray for our enemies, and reach out to those in need. As we do what His heart desires, we conform to His image and not the world's. Maybe we are not as cute as little ducklings, but humble, empowered, and loving, we can be as beautiful at the core as Christ.

Jesus, lead in Your loving ways, and I will follow as
a duckling paddles behind its mother. Transform my
heart along the way to look like Yours. Amen.

FISHING-ROD PATIENCE

Be still before the LORD
and wait patiently for him.

PSALM 37:7

S itting in a small fishing boat under fair skies, you hook a worm. You swing the fishing rod behind you and then forward, gently releasing the line. The worm soars over the water with the line wiggling behind its lead. There's a small splash, rippling, and then the water goes still again.

Now you wait. It's nice sitting back in the boat knowing you've done your part for now. It's peaceful, and you relax into sitting, waiting, watching. Until you feel a tug.

This isn't your first fish hunt and you recognize the short, light pull of a tease. But the almost-catch causes your patience to waver.

Know that feeling? When we are waiting on God, the almost-delivery of a promise can shake us out of our patience. In those times, we can remind ourselves of God's faithfulness and that His best is worth waiting for even in the disappointments of the "almosts."

Before long, the line will tug firmly and you will reel in the real catch. In the meantime, sit back in your boat and enjoy the stillness.

God, in the waiting to catch Your promises and
gifts, grow in me patience and peace. Amen.

ICE-CREAM DROPS

Delight yourself in the LORD,
and he will give you the desires of your heart.

PSALM 37:4 ESV

Bubblegum, chocolate peanut butter, strawberry cheesecake: flavors of ice cream pile up high on your cone. It's a hot day by the lake and drops of colors stick to the grass around you, drips that fall faster than you can lick. Whatever favorite flavors you choose, ice cream is a delight.

To delight in something means we find joy and satisfaction in it. Indulging in the cold, refreshing sweetness of ice cream is a pleasure unmatched by any other sunny-day snack. God actually invites us to delight in Him. Close communion with our Father is a pleasure for our hearts that we can find nowhere else.

Great news: we cannot overindulge in the goodness of God! His sweetness dribbles and overflows, and we have more than enough to fill our hearts. He knows which flavors of ice cream are our favorites just as He knows all the dearest desires of our hearts. He won't hold back from piling our cones high when we take delight in Him.

Father, teach me to find my joy and satisfaction in You. I
want my life to be dripping with Your goodness. Amen.

BONFIRE FRIENDS

It has seemed good to me to show the signs and wonders
that the Most High God has done for me.

DANIEL 4:2 ESV

Smoky fireside smells, sticky s'more ingredients, and crackling flames popping in a pile of wood welcome friends comfortably around a bonfire at the lake. Trees line one side of the grassy opening with the lake bordering the other. The water carries into the dark distance, meeting the stars that stud the inky sky over the group huddled in a circle around the fire pit.

The glow around the blaze mesmerizes each member and a hush falls on the group. Moments pass with everyone in a retrospective mind-set until someone says, "One time, when I was younger. . . ." One by one memories surface and are shared within this sacred space of trusted friends.

The narratives of our lives are complex and mysterious. Our winding roads create grooves in our hearts and shape our minds in ways we don't even realize. When we talk them out with close friends, the perplexing parts can become clearer and our friends can offer fresh insight and encouragement. When we open up to a devoted community in our lives, we have the chance to be better known and therefore better loved.

God draws us to Himself first, and then to our right and left we will find friends in our circle whom we can trust with the deeper parts of our stories. They become our bonfire friends. Like Daniel we can share with them "the signs and wonders" of our lives lived with God.

*Father, draw me to You and connect me with bonfire
friends so I can gain depth of understanding
of my story and who I am in You. Amen.*

STILLNESS OF A HERON

"Be still, and know that I am God."

PSALM 46:10

D own by a creek leading to the lake, a great blue heron stands balancing on one leg on a log. The bird's elongated body with sleek feathers down its back seems frozen in its stock-still position. Even if the water bubbles up or trees sway strongly in the wind, the heron has the uncanny ability to stay completely still.

When we are surrounded by changing, animated situations with far-reaching decisions to make, we can be still before God. Of course, not many of us have the physical balance to stand unmoving on one leg by a flowing creek with wind in the air. Rather it is in the posture of our hearts and minds toward God when circumstances are shifting like the weather: if we stop our anxious thoughts and steady our beating hearts, we can be quiet before God and bring to the forefront the knowledge that He is sovereign, He is Creator, and He is Controller of the conditions swirling around us. The knowing steadies our hearts and minds so we can rest before God as still as a heron.

God, help me grasp the truth of Your sovereignty in my life and find a heron's stillness in the knowing. Amen.

WHEN LIFE MOVES TOO FAST

"Abide in my love."

JOHN 15:9 ESV

The best spot on a boat is in the back, where you can stretch out on the long, cushioned seat. The sun is beating down on you, but the boat's speed causes a continual breeze to blow through your hair, keeping you cool. It's a rush to be traveling at such a high speed while reclined and sunbathing. The lakeshore whizzes by.

Even though the boat is moving quickly, you are relaxed and steady. Sometimes events in our lives get accelerated: plans go forward before we feel ready, and life seems to fly by like the scenery on the lake bank. Sometimes God speeds things up to get us where we need to be. When life seems to be zipping out of control, we can hold our spots and trust the Driver.

God will slow the boat down in other seasons, but when it's time to kick it up a notch, we can enjoy the ride and the breeze in our hair without looking back. Even though the scenery flying by is beautiful and we may feel a twinge of loss to miss it, we wouldn't dream of reaching out to grab ahold of a branch. Instead, we let it all go and know that where we are headed will be even better. When those fast-forward seasons come in life, remember to hold your spot in the back of the boat and stay relaxed in trust.

God, when life seems to be moving too quickly, keep me settled in my spot in the boat with You to enjoy the ride. I trust where You are taking me is even better than anything going by. Amen.

THE MISNAMED DRAGONFLY

There is no fear in love, but perfect love casts out fear.

1 JOHN 4:18 ESV

Despite the danger implied in the dragonfly's name, these aquatic bugs living near our lakes and ponds do not sting or bite; they are completely harmless to humans. Sometimes they curl their long, stick-like bodies in pretense as if poised to sting, but this is only a stunt. Don't be alarmed if one alights near you. Instead, enjoy its vibrant colors and observe its patterned wings that give it the remarkable ability to move forward, backward, up, and down and to hover, like a helicopter.

Sometimes the most fascinating, wonderful gifts frighten us the most. For example, a romantic relationship, a dream job, or an artistic accomplishment: whatever it is we highly desire and prize can fill us with fear because we might fail or lose it once we gain it. But like the intimidation some people feel about a dragonfly due to its name, the fear is a fake-out. It's a mirage of the worst-case scenario that takes away peace and fills us with dread of loss, rejection, or defeat, keeping us from the very blessings God has ordained for us as His children.

God's love existed even before the dragonflies and has the ability to drive out anything that frightens us from our good inheritance. Fear creates illusions; God's love is real.

Father, when I am afraid, show me Your perfect
love for me that replaces fear. Amen.

FISH FRY

Jesus said to them, "Come and have breakfast."

JOHN 21:12 ESV

The scene happened on the shore of a lake. The disciples had returned to their business of fishing after the tragedy that had taken place on a cross-shadowed hill. Then a man strode onto the shore and told the disciples to try fishing on the other side of the boat. Immediately fish swarmed into the nets and the disciples caught a haul so big they couldn't drag it into the boat. Peter's memory flashed back to the same occurrence when he first met Jesus (Luke 5:6), and knowing it was the Lord on the shore, he jumped into the water and swam toward the risen Savior.

Once all the disciples arrived onshore, the first thing Jesus said to them wasn't to go and save the world or to do big things for the kingdom. The first thing He said was to come and eat. Gathering around the freshly prepared bread and fish, the disciples marveled at the scar-marked hands breaking the bread and the familiar, kind eyes meeting theirs. The men were all seen, known, loved, and served by the Lord *before* He gave the Great Commission to go and make disciples of all nations (Matthew 28:19).

Jesus told the disciples, as He tells us, that if we follow Him He makes us fishers of men, winning hearts for the kingdom. But before this, He sits with us, looks us in the eye, and feeds us. Jesus cares about spending time with us before He sends us out to accomplish anything for the day or the kingdom. That is the start: a hearty breakfast with our Lord.

Jesus, each morning let me savor Your presence with me. Prepare me for my great calling to draw others to Your table. Amen.

THE GOLDEN HOUR

*For his invisible attributes, namely, his eternal power and divine
nature, have been clearly perceived, ever since the creation
of the world, in the things that have been made.*

ROMANS 1:20 ESV

The last hour of daylight, when the sun is nearing the edge of the horizon, creates a magical frame for creation. The sun's low angle on the earth gives its light a softer touch with a warming radiance spreading over all of nature. The golden glow falls on the grass, glints on the leaves, and glimmers over the lake water. It is said that the streets of heaven are paved with gold; can they be more beautiful than this?

When we stop to savor the sunset and enter a moment of reflection, we see how every part of our day—not just sunset—carried a connection to heaven. All of creation reflects God's glory, including our menial tasks of daily life: cooking, cleaning, working, caring for children, running errands, resting. Each simple act can express the love of Christ, which harmoniously binds everything together.

When each day is winding down and the sky is darkening after brilliant color, let's let the divine inscription on each passed moment cast a golden glow and embrace the entirety in heaven's hold.

*Father, when I look back over my day, let me
see the golden glory of heaven that was present
and glimmering in every moment. Amen.*